This book is a peep through the multiple doors that the author has passed in the course of his career. The account is a product of history. Guided by historical actuality, the author focuses on factuality, authenticity and the true value of knowledge in his reflections about the past. There is no myth or legend in the book. What we have is living history. Even though the author tries to navigate the book out of the realm of autobiography, he, nonetheless, embarks upon a historical narrative that pieces together the rudiments of yesterday and converts them into raw materials for present engagement. The blend is uncommon. It exemplifies and highlights the eclectic bent of the author as an accomplished raconteur. His adoption of the historical approach in his narrative is significant. It has helped to identify the author as an artist with a significant past and a predisposition to write in a certain manner. This knowledge enables the reader to ascertain how the book reflects the historical forces that shaped it. It has also enabled us to understand how the historical moment upon which the book is anchored produced the moving tale that the author has told. This knowledge guides us into acknowledging the fact that the author's experiences in whatever field he has traversed are not his alone. Instead, they have a universal appeal that makes the account not just the author's story, but everyone's story.

Dr. Amanze Obi, scholar, writer and journalist, was educated at the University of Lagos. He spent eleven unbroken years in the university and bagged multiple degrees, capping it with a doctorate in English. He taught in the department of English of the University of Lagos in the early years of his career. A front-line journalist and celebrated columnist with over three decades of media exposure, Obi has worked with major Nigerian newspapers where he held senior editorial positions. His weekly newspaper column, BROKEN TONGUES, is easily the toast of perspective readers. Obi was, at various times, Commissioner for Information and Strategy as well as that of Culture and Tourism in Imo State. He was also the pioneer Director General of the Ahiajoku Institute ,the think tank on Igbo worldview and civilization. He is the author of PERSPECTIVES IN INTERNATIONAL POLITICS (1998) and DELICATE DISTRESS: An Interpreter's account of the Nigerian Dilemma (2013).

SCENTS
of
POWER

SCENTS *of* POWER

My Personal Encounters with
Power and Influence

DR. AMANZE OBI

Copyright 2022 by Gr8 Entity Ltd UK

All rights reserved. No part of this book may be reproduced or used in any manner without written permission of the copyright owner except for the use of quotations in a book review.

ISBNs:
Paperback: 978-1-80227-490-5
eBook: 978-1-80227-491-2
Hardback: 978-1-80227-839-2

CONTENTS

Acknowledgments vii
Foreword ix
Introduction xi

PART ONE: THE UNIVERSITY YEARS

1. A Freshman on Campus 2
2. Campus Politics 9
3. Climbing the Pole 19
4. Starting a Doctorate 23

PART TWO: THE NEWSPAPER YEARS

5. From the Guardian to Thisday 33
6. The Interregnum 37
7. Voyage to Congo 43
8. A Revolution under Threat 55
9. Birth of Broken Tongues 63
10. Bride of The Sun 71
11. Creating The Sun Back Page Column 75
12. Travelling for The Sun 77
13. At Home with Mandela 83
14. Going to America 91

15. Land of Lincoln 95
16. In Retrospect 99

PART THREE: GOVERNMENT AND POLITICS

17. Dawn of Democracy 103
18. In the Purgatory 115
19. A Dark Horse Marches In 123
20. Age of Innocence 131
21. The Honey Moon 135
22. The Kalu-Ohakim Wedger 147
23. The Lull Begins 161
24. The Last Straw 165
25. After the Fall 171
26. Enter the Machine God 175
27. Reality Sets In 183
28. Photo Finish 187
29. Politics Nigeriana 191
30. My Political Baptism 201
31. Practical Politics 207
32. Pioneering the Ahiajoku Institute 217
33. A Touchstone for the Festival 225

Postscript 233
Notes and References 241
About the Book 243
About the Author 245
Name Index 247
Subject Index 251

ACKNOWLEDGEMENTS

The making of this book was slow but steady. I slowed down on the project a couple of times for reasons that border on political expediency. But my association with His Excellency, the governor of Kano State, Dr Abdullahi Umar Ganduje, served as the elixir that I needed to break away from strictures and constraints. The ideas we shared were invaluable at the completion stages of this book. To underline his support for the project, His Excellency, in spite of his very busy schedule as the chief executive of a complex state like Kano, found time to write the Foreword to this book. Your Excellency, I owe you a debt of gratitude for your interest and commitment to this project.

Let me state, for the avoidance of doubt, that my relationship with the three masters that I served under formed the fulcrum of this book. Each of them gave me reason to embark on this project. Prince Nduka Obaigbena injected in me the spirit of daring and independent journalism. His Excellency, Orji Uzor Kalu, gave me remarkable international exposure in the course of my career. His Excellency, Ikedi Ohakim, gave me a chance. He called me to serve without prompting. I am grateful to these three gentlemen for inspiring me in various ways.

Bidwell Nsofor, the man with an eye for detail, came in handy when I needed someone with whom to share my thoughts about this book. He not only served as my in-house editor, he provided useful guides that saw to the maturation and actualisation of the book. Thanks, Brother Bidwell.

Prof. Andrew Okwilagbe and his team of editors at Stirling-Horden Publishers Ltd., made this book a better product. I thank them for their professionalism.

Silverline Ngozi served as my networking and logistics officer. She ensured proper mobilization, coordination and implementation.

My wife, Chinyere, who is always my first and last line of defence, was always there to spur me into action. On a number of occasions, she graciously granted me sabbatical leave in order for me to concentrate on the project. Thank you my jewel for your understanding and enormous sacrifice.

To all others who supported this project one way or the other, I thank you all.

FOREWORD

The most important role journalists play in society is setting the agenda for discourse on development. That explains why beyond reporting news, the more enlightened ones ruminate and speak out over sensitive national issues, thereby enabling the country to discuss the issues dispassionately, highlighting all the available perspectives and leading to a national consensus.

The media is addressed as the Fourth Estate of the Realm for a reason; they report, analyze and critique the clergy, the nobility and the commoners according to the traditional British concept , but now, this role seems to have shifted to government officials in the executive, legislature and the judiciary at the federal, state and local levels. A little more introspection and action on the traditional concept is important at this time.

Even with the spread of unregulated online media, to which membership does not require competence, the journalists have remained, largely, an embodiment of responsible reporting, abiding by the rules and guidelines of their profession. I hope that journalists will continue to imbue this agenda-setting role to strengthen national cohesion, expose corruption and loopholes in the system as well as recommend areas for further development especially economic and political.

Dr. Amanze Obi is a journalist that has traversed the media landscape and made his imprint in many national dailies; his opinion has found favour in the public domain, adding value to the papers' image and economics. He got a chance to walk his talk when he got appointed to serve as a commissioner on two occasions. His claim therefore that he only scented power is very modest, to say the least; he tasted power. The title of this book therefore should have been Taste of Power.

I do believe that this autobiography will conscript many journalists into his journey, enabling them to carve their paths along the lines of professionalism, patriotism and activism.

Dr Abdullahi Umar Ganduje
Governor of Kano State
March, 2021.

INTRODUCTION

Power is one of the most central, yet ironically problematic, concepts in sociological theory. It is loosely regarded as the capacity of an individual to influence the conduct or behaviour of others. Scholars have, over time, espoused on the concept of power. In their various inquiries, they have gone beyond the common, everyday encapsulation of the concept.

One of the scholars who have put a stamp of authority on the protean colourations of power is Maximilian Karl Emil Weber, otherwise known as Max Weber. Weber, a German sociologist, philosopher, jurist and political economist who lived between 1864 and 1920, defines power as "the ability of an individual or group to achieve their own goals or aims when others are trying to prevent them from realising them."[1] He also sees power as the ability to exercise one's will over others. Power does not just affect personal relationships; it shapes larger dynamics like social groups, professional organisations and governments. Weber categorizes power as either authoritative or coercive. Whereas authoritative power is seen as legitimate because those who are subject to such power do so consensually, coercion is the exercise of power through force. In other words, the use of power is at the discretion of the one who possesses it.

While the likes of Weber were concerned about the sociology of power, some other theorists were more practical. They were rather interested in the actual use to which people in positions of authority put power. One such person is John Emerich Edward Dalberg Acton (1834-1902), simply known as Lord Acton. In 1887, Acton had cause to write Bishop Mandell Creighton, historian and Bishop of London. In the letter, Acton, an English historian and moralist, held that "power tends to corrupt, and absolute power corrupts absolutely. Great men are almost always bad men."[2] The letter was, in part, Acton's espousal on historical integrity. He had rejected the canon that we are to judge Pope and King unlike other men, with a favourable presumption that they did no wrong. Acton's thesis was part of a larger conversation about how historians should judge the past and how the role of men of power and influence shapes societies.

Acton was not really the first to express deep worries about the possible damage absolute power can do or is capable of doing to society as well as to its wielders. Before him, William Pitt the Elder, Earl of Chatham and British Prime Minister from 1766-1778, had said something similar. In a speech in 1770 to the United Kingdom House of Lords, Pitt said: "Unlimited power is apt to corrupt the minds of those who possess it, and this I know, my lords, that where law ends, tyranny begins."[3]

In contemporary times, theorists on power also exist. One of the most prominent is Robert Greene, an American author known for his books on strategy, power and seduction. His best-selling book, "The 48 Laws of Power", has been described by THE TIMES (of London) as the companion for those who want power, watch power, or want to arm themselves against power.

Power, according to Greene, "is essentially amoral and one of the most important skills to acquire is the ability to see circumstances rather than good or evil. Power is a game- this cannot be repeated too often- and in games you do not judge your opponents by their intentions but by the effect of their actions."[4] For Greene as well, "power is endlessly seductive and deceptive in its own way. It is a labyrinth- your mind becomes consumed with solving its infinite problems, and you soon realise how pleasantly lost you have become."[5]

Indeed, power and the use to which it is put have, from time immemorial, been a source of concern to mankind. In monarchical settings, absolute power is usually concentrated in the hands of an authority. A case in point is that of Roman Emperors who declared themselves gods and rode roughshod over their subjects.

The fear of the danger inherent in absolute power may not have derived from these worries and experiences. But society has, nonetheless, been bedeviled by issues that have to do with absolute power. However, and gratifyingly too, modern democracies have put in place institutional checks and balances that make reckless and absolute display or deployment of power not the norm but an exception. This notwithstanding, societies, organisations and individuals have continued to come under the corroding influence of power and its wielders.

My career path, over the years, has been marked by encounters with men of power and influence. The use they made or did not make of power affected me, one way or another. They played a role in shaping my perception. The experience, for me, is like a leit motif. It is the rhythm to which my recollections are subjected. It is like the keynote in a symphony to which the strange melody always returns. What I render in this book therefore is a distillation of select events in my career progression which, if I should assume the role of an Everyman, can qualify as a universal story. The account is essentially semi-autobiographical. What we have here therefore is not just my story. It is everyone's story. Indeed, our story.

Part One
The University Years

Chapter 1

A FRESHMAN ON CAMPUS

The most memorable years of my coming of age began in 1984. That was the year I commenced my undergraduate studies at the University of Lagos. I had, in December of that year, arrived the University campus fresh and uncorrupted. I was hardly familiar with anyone on campus, having come from the Eastern axis of the country where I had my secondary school education. There were no classmates or schoolmates from my secondary school that I knew of at the point of entry. I was, however, to discover a few of my secondary school mates on campus months or years later. But there were really no acquaintances at the very beginning. I started on a new and fresh note.

However, no sooner had I arrived campus than like minds began to flock together. In no time, I became a member of a circle of friends whose utmost interest on campus was to discover the world of books. Whereas the undergraduate class was, at that time, awash with juvenile enthusiasts who lacked the cognitive sense to put persons and characters in a straitjacket, my friends saw beyond surface, plastic reality. They were in the habit of formulating tales and painting pictures in order to capture certain realities that may not be obvious to many. Within a few months of our union, I was, for whatever reason, to become the most discussed individual among them.

Douglas Anele, now a Professor of Philosophy at the University of Lagos, led the team of friends who felt that I was an intriguing personality. He had ready supporters in Kingsley Nwankwo and Benedict Kentebe who found my ways both amusing and enthralling. They saw my ways as easy-going and unobtrusive, especially in my dealings with women. They said I exhibited tendencies that border on the unserious. Yet, beyond that veneer of unseriousness lay a firm spirit and a focused personality who did not brook any nonsense. Such a curious mix thrilled them. As the years went by, their impressions about me became crystallized into what was later to be christened "The Dr. Amanze Obi Phenomenon". By the time we spent some three years in the University, the Phenomenon had assumed a life of its own. It became articulated into a document of sorts. At graduation, the Phenomenon had become a clear and unambiguous document. It reads thus:

"The Dr. Amanze Obi Phenomenon is not an attempt at myth-making. It is no legendary either. On the contrary, it is an attempt at a realistic explication of the essence of an otherwise misconceived personality. A man highly misunderstood, Dr. Amanze Obi represents to most people the best and basest of human motives ominously interwoven in him. Because he is imbued with a mind boundless in all its aspirations and unceasing in its compulsions, he is dismissed in some quarters as a slave of phantoms. But he has methodically belied this impression, riding the crest in a manner that usually leaves his detractors gaping. Like a Romantic Hero, his striving is to elevate himself above the common herd of his environment with the sheer scope of his imagination.

But unlike him (the Romantic hero) he does not have contempt for the prosaic trivia of day-to-day existence.

"In academic matters, he is either seen as a 'rigour major' or a 'layabout'. But he is neither here nor there. Rather, he tends towards a balance. Like Jane Austin, he believes that balance is a prime virtue to be aimed at. A language connoisseur, he always proves his mettle in matters of logic and commonsense, using realistic analyses to supplant romantic incantations. Like Jane Fairfax in Highbury, he is regarded in academic circles as an intellectual recluse whose presence makes everybody else feel inadequate. He enjoys literary flourishes and fine phrases.

"He is one of the bearers of the Forsterian Virtues – the virtues of the developed hearts, of spontaneous passion, and of trust in the imagination. Being of this mould, he does battle with the armies of the benighted who follow neither the heart nor the brain. He regards political speech as an abstraction that generates pious lies. Politicians are, for him, masters of ghost words. He considers these reprehensible. This neatly accounts for his occasional forays into students unionism, for he shares the view of Alexander Pope that the reign of the prince of evil terminates in universal darkness.

"The prima donnas of his environment act as a jinx in his affairs. When it is not the prima donnas, it is the ravishing ladies with seductive ambience, the blue stockings and the femme fatales. This is one stigma he fights relentlessly to keep at bay, but it has stuck deep into his love fabric. However, he has come out of many of such engagements unscathed. This success story is not unconnected with his incurable chariness about women.

"Then, there is this tag of 'self-opinionated' being placed on him. To see him in this light is to display an abysmal ignorance of the stuff he is made of. He is essentially an individual who shuns stereotypes. Like a true romantic, he adores the individual. He is not ruled by the opinion of the crowd, for he believes that the majority may not necessarily be right. Some see this as an act of self righteousness. This is a wrong notion of him. Perhaps, the best way to encapsulate him in this regard is to say that like William Blake, he believes in constructing his own system rather that play the slave to other people's systems. "This ability to stem the tide, to keep afloat in the face of the rough storm, to belie the expectations of arm-chair critics and mischief-makers, and to retain his sanity in the face of flurries of mind-boggling siege mentality is astonishingly admirable. Even the most virulent of his glib critics agree that he is carving a niche in the temple of fame. It is in this that the essential AMANZE lies. This is the DR. AMANZE OBI phenomenon".

This was essentially the way I was packaged and sold among my circle of friends on campus. This impression of me, whatever its pitfalls may be, possibly captures my essential personality. Issues arising from it have affected, and in some cases, infected those who associated with me, one way or another. In fact, my friends' depiction of my personality derived largely from their everyday encounters with me. At the University of Lagos of our era, two campus slangs defined every student. You were either a "rigour major" or a "layabout". Rigour majors were academic devotees who detested or almost detested any engagement that is extra curricular. They were not interested in the social or political life on campus. They minded nothing but their books. Layabouts were the direct opposite of rigour majors. It referred to students who paid very little attention to their studies. Such students were found more at social gatherings than in lecture halls. Their academic pursuits were laidback. Their attraction on campus tended more towards social life than to their books. They almost loathed academic engagements.

I was, curiously, associated with both lifestyles. The reason was not far-fetched. I participated actively in students union politics. I also paid more than a cursory attention to social activities. I was a known face in many of the night clubs that dotted the Lagos landscape then. In fact, I came close to being a Disc Jockey, a lifestyle I was attracted to during my secondary school days. I just love engaging the microphone in a hilarious manner. Based on this, those who found me in such circles did not think that I was a serious-minded student. But the reality, on the contrary, was that I was among the outstanding academic performers in the University. I was easily the brightest student in my class. I wrote essays that my lecturers never failed to acknowledge as bright and brilliant. To those who followed my outstanding academic performance, I was nothing but a rigour major. That was the curious mix in me that my friends found intriguing.

Chapter 2

CAMPUS POLITICS

I developed interest in campus politics in my first year in the university. Students union elections provided a lot of excitement and side attractions on campus during our time. The 1985 exercise paraded aspirants who knew the history of the University well enough. They regaled us with what they knew about the university. Some of us who were freshmen were thrilled. We were even more thrilled by the Marxist indulgences of some of the candidates. It was fashionable on campus at that time to dress in a certain bohemian manner and reel out what you know or pretend to know about Leninism-Marxism. Such Marxist pretensions were part of the hallmarks that marked students union activists out. Even though I was not taken in by the sociological abstractions that the activists indulged in, I, nonetheless, loved the gyrations and hall-to-hall campaigns.

By the time my first year ended, I had taken sufficient interest in students union politics. Thus, in my second year, I was elected into the University of Lagos Students Union (ULSU) parliament. A certain Moshood Fayemiwo popularly known as "Fayee" was the president of the students union then. Fayee, a very eloquent activist, was the toast of many students on campus at the time. His level of social exposure was higher than that of an average student. He made tremendous impact on the psyche of many students.

They loved him for his oratory and measured radicalism. That was why he was given the mandate by his fellow students to mount the saddle as the president of the students union.

Regrettably, he could not serve out his tenure. In the course of his tenure as ULSU president, he was accused of certain wrongdoings that the parliament could not ignore. Consequently, he was impeached, and he fell from Olympian Heights. In fact, one of the most remarkable events that took place at ULSU parliament in the 1985/86 session was the impeachment of Fayee as the students union president.

After my one year tenure at ULSU parliament, I returned to my department and was elected the President of English Students Association for the 1986/87 session. Within the same period, I was also elected the President of National Association of Students of English Language and Literature (NASELL). Under my presidency, NASELL held its 3rd National Conference at UNILAG from January 22nd – 23rd, 1988. Representatives of students of English Language and Literature from virtually all Nigerian Universities attended the conference. It was an intellectual harvest at which participants from various universities showcased their linguistic and literary prowess. As the president, much was expected of me. Fortunately, I had more than a mouthful for my colleagues. I started by welcoming them with an academic paper on semantics and sociolinguistics which sought to establish a nexus between meaning and culture. Aspects of the paper read as follows:

"Semanticists have given various but related definitions to the word 'Meaning'. They seem to agree that the meaning of 'Meaning' is difficult to pin-point.

While it is not within the province of this paper to go into such discussions, John Lyons's definition of meaning shall be adopted as a paradigm in this essay.

"For Lyons, "Meanings are ideas or concepts which can be transferred from the mind of the speaker to the mind of the hearer by embodying them, as it were, in the forms of one language or another."[6]

"Like meaning, Culture has several definitions. There are some conceptions of culture as developed by Herder which border on the classical and the anthropological. These are, however, not relevant for our present purpose. We shall again take recourse to John Lyons's definition of culture as a socially acquired knowledge, that is, the knowledge that someone has by virtue of his being a member of a particular society.

"J.R. Firth, who developed the theory of meaning tells us that it (meaning) is closely tied to culture. Every utterance, he says, occurs in a culturally-determined context of situation, and that the meaning of an utterance is the totality of its contribution to the maintenance of what he refers to as the patterns of life in the society in which the speaker lives.

"Firth's thesis leads us to the understanding that voice quality, for instance, is part of the mode of meaning of any speaker. This is so because voice quality is culturally acquired. Thus, it can be stated that it is part of the meaning for a Yoruba, for instance, to sound like one.

"Such statements as these are not intended to involve us in coarse and wilful extension of the meaning of meaning. They are, on the contrary, consistent with Firth's general views that to be meaningful or having meaning is a matter of functioning appropriately or significantly in context.

"Thus, to speak for instance, with an Igbo accent of English is to indicate that one is an Igbo and in so far as speaking with an Igbo accent is the result of one's socialization as an Igbo, it makes sense to say that in speaking with an Igbo accent, one is simultaneously being an Igbo and meaning that one is an Igbo.

"This point can be looked at from a social and behavioural point of view. Here, we note that one's modes of being (which derive from one's culture), are one's modes of meaning; and one means what one is by behaving in such and such a way in one's context. In this sense, meaning can be said to be intrinsically linked with culture.

"The key word in the Firthian theory of meaning is 'context'. Thus, the analysis of the meaning of an utterance will consist, as he put it, in "a serial contextualization of our facts. Context within context, each one being a function, an organ of the bigger context and all contexts finding a place in what might be called the context of culture."[7]

"Firth's appeal here to the context of culture is simply a recognition of the intimate connection between language and culture. This leads us to the realization that language utterances, like other bits of socially significant bahaviour, could not be interpreted otherwise than by conceptualizing them in relation to a particular culture.

"The Sapir-Whorf hypothesis can be used to explain the notion of meaning and culture. The hypothesis combines linguistic determinism ("language determines thoughts") with linguistic relativity ("there is no limit to the structural diversity of languages"). The main thesis of the idea is that we are in all our thinking, "at the mercy of the particular language which has become the medium of expression of our society,"[8] because we cannot but "see and hear and otherwise experience"[9] in terms of the categories and distinctions encoded in language. It also stipulates that the categories of distinctions encoded in one language-system are unique to that system and incommensurable with those of other systems.

"We can relate this hypothesis to the notion of culture and meaning. It is generally agreed that memory and perception are affected by the availability of appropriate words and expressions. Experience has shown that people tend to notice and remember the things that are codable in their language, that is, the things that fall within the scope of readily available words and expressions.

What is not codable in one's language has no meaning in that language and as such a stranger to that culture, for if there is affinity between that code and the culture, then it must be meaningful in that speech-community.

"The thesis of linguistic relativity as propounded by the theory is relevant to the issue at stake. This is because many of the differences of grammatical and lexical structure found in language (they determine meaning) are such that some things that can be said in one language cannot be said in another language. By extension, it means that those things that cannot be said in that language have no meaning in the said language and thus irrelevant to the culture in which that language operates.

"The examination of the relationship between meaning and culture still points to another salient fact – that is that language is a cultural phenomenon. It is noteworthy that linguistic competence is transmitted from one generation to the next by means of a particular society's institutions, and that what is transmitted is itself an important component in that society's culture.

"Thus, if competence in a particular language implies the ability to understand sentences of that language, then competence is a part of culture, that is, social knowledge. This is so because much of the meaning of expressions, including their descriptive as well as their social and expressive meaning, is culture-dependent.

"In fact, full understanding of the several kinds of meaning that are encoded in the grammar and vocabulary of a language comes only with a full understanding of the culture, or cultures, in which it operates.

"Variants in the conventions of politeness as we move from one culture to the other also bring to focus the relationship between the concepts under study.

What is polite in one language situation may not be so in another. This is tied to the meaning which every language group attaches to words and expressions. "Another way of putting it is to say that modes of verbal behaviour, which is meaning-dependent, differs from one linguistic culture to another. For instance, most Nigerian linguistic cultures are gerontocratic. In this vein, one does not just address one's elder as 'Paul' or 'Mr. Paul'. There is always a sobriquet attached to the name depending on the culture. In Igbo English for instance, it is considered rude for an adult to address somebody of his parent's age group by his or her name. You would rather address such a person as 'father', 'mother' as the case may be, or use the name of any of his children. For example, you may say 'Ngozi's father'.

"Issues bordering on sex-education also bring to focus the relationship between meaning and culture. For instance, the Nigerian culture is one that attaches much importance to such issues. While the English and most Europeans will discuss sex-education freely among the adolescents and the adults, Nigerians, whether literate or not will not. To us in Nigeria, such mundane discussions are considered vulgar and as such a taboo. This is due to the meaning we attach to such issues, and such meaning derives from our cultural mould. This shows that even though we share the use of the English Language with the English people, we do not share the same sociolinguistic rules of usage.

"The point being stressed here is that a language or words of a language cannot be either good or bad but can only be seen as such by the people who use it.

One word may have positive connotation while another with identical meaning may have negative connotation. Fromkin and Bodman (1978) say that "Language cannot be sexist in itself, just as it cannot be "dirty", but it can reflect sexist attitudes just as to what is or what is not "taboo".[10]

Consider for instance, the sentence. My cousin is a nurse.

"A statement like this will send most Nigerians thinking that the cousin in question is a woman because nursing is a profession in which women form the majority. Thus, one talks of male nurse because it is expected that a nurse will always be female. It is for the same reason that we have parallels like lady doctor, lady cobbler, lady watch-maker and so on.

"It is for the same sexist bias in the use of language that United Bank for Africa (U.B.A) which used to advertise with the catchphrase which says that "wise men bank with U.B.A", now has the adjunct "and women too". The attachment of those sexual asymmetries to meaning is culturally-derived.

"Perhaps, the best way to conclude this essay is to say that language is conceptualized as a socially conditioned product and as such it should be congruent with certain social expectations from people who belong to certain attitudes and such social attitudes derive from culture".

The presentation of this paper was the opening salvo that set the stage for the NASELL conference in 1988. At the end of my presentation, it became clear to participants that they were in for a true intellectual exercise. Those who thought they had come to have fun girded their loins. More presentations came from other participants. We had an intellectually fulfilling day. The second day of the conference was equally engaging. But when we retired to the bar session on that second day, I presented the gathering with some intelligent quotes and wise banters for discussion. Some of the brain teasers read like this:

1. Attempt an interpretation and analysis of the proposition of the ascetics that love reveals our shameful kinship with beasts.
2. Life is unmanageable because it is a romance. But its essence is romantic beauty. How plausible is this contention?

3. How true is it to propose that to trust people is a luxury in which only the rich can indulge; the poor cannot afford it?
4. Comment on the statement of Dr. Johnson that he that is discovered without his own consent, may claim some indulgence, and cannot be rigorously called to justify those sallies or frolicks which his disguise is a proof that he wishes to conceal.
5. Evaluate the contention that until you have got a true theory of humanity, you cannot interpret history and when you have got a true theory of humanity you do not want history.
6. How logical is it to say that if human nature is the highest nature to men, then practically also the highest and first law must be the love of man to man?
7. A wife is a constituted check on her husband's pleasures. Discuss.
8. People who seem to enjoy their ill-temper have a way of keeping it in fine condition by inflicting privations on themselves. Is this true of human nature?
9. We can seldom declare what a thing is except by saying it is something else. Discuss.
10. Matrimony, like death, is a leap in the dark. How plausible is this view? These wise cracks brought out the best in the participants. Discussing them presented the students the opportunity to demonstrate how knowledgeable they were. The conference left lasting impressions on the minds of students of English and Literature who were at the event. It was, without doubt, the highpoint of my one-year reign as the president of NASELL.

By July 1988, I graduated from UNILAG, emerging as the best graduating student in the Department of English of the University with Second Class Honours (Upper Division). I was rewarded with the Dean's award for best performance in a subject within a teaching unit. In September of the same year, I was deployed to Akwa Ibom State for the National Youth Service Corps (NYSC) scheme. My service year ended in August 1989 and I returned to UNILAG immediately for my Masters degree programme.

Chapter 3

CLIMBING THE POLE

While pursuing my higher degree, I chose a career path. I wanted to be a journalist. My choice of the career was in line with what I love doing most - writing. By that time, I had resolved the initial conflict in me between writing and speaking. Speech has always had a thrilling effect on me. That explains my initial predilection towards being a Disc Jockey. But writing also had its hold on me. Literature, as a matter of fact, sharpened my love for the written word. I needed to go either way. But as I grew older, I told myself that writing will be a more enduring engagement for me. That was how it all began. Having made up my mind as to what I wanted, I did not have to jump from one office to the other in search of job opportunities. I simply sat back on campus, focused on my Masters degree programme but occasionally found time also to contribute articles to various newspapers in Lagos.

In the course of my freelance contributions to newspapers, I had encountered a fine gentleman called Ely Obasi. He was an editor at Newswatch magazine then. Mr. Tom Anaduaka, a staff of Vanguard Newspapers whom I knew way back in the early 1980s while he was with the Punch Newspapers, introduced me to Ely. Soon afterwards, Ely and I became intellectual companions. Ely cherished and respected men of intellect. He was to leave Newswatch shortly after our acquaintance in search of better opportunities.

There were no mobile telephones in Nigeria at the time. So, I lost contact with him. But we were reunited at The Sunday Magazine (TSM) published by Mrs Chris Anyanwu. I joined Ely and the enterprising TSM team in July 1990. That was the beginning of my formal career in journalism. I still recall that first week I spent at TSM. The story for that week was the demolition of Marako, a sprawling slum on the bank of the Atlantic Ocean, by the Lagos State Government under the administration of Col. Raji Rasaki. Marako was a huge slum that gazed at affluence represented by Victoria Island and Ikoyi. The mix between these opposites did not speak well of a Lagos that the government of the day dreamt of. Also, Marako was becoming a risky settlement because of incessant flooding from the Atlantic Ocean. The then Military government of Raji Rasaki took the bold step to reclaim Marako from its slum status. It demolished the enclave. Hundreds of thousands of people were displaced in the process.

My job at TSM came at the time the second semester of my Masters degree programme just began. The magazine which normally hit the newstand on Sundays was produced on Wednesdays. More often than not, the production stretched through Wednesday night to about midday of Thursday. All editorial and production staff were required, as a rule, to sleep in the office on production days.

This production schedule did not suit my lecture time table for the Masters class. It clashed with one of my courses – Modern Drama – which held every Thursday from 9am to 12noon. The clash posed enormous challenge to me. The semester had just begun; and the job had just started. I could not abandon production. My absence would be too obvious. I agonized over this. At some point, I had to confide in one of the staff, Rita Ese Edah, who had graduated three years before me from the Department of English of the University of Lagos. I had sought her advice on whether

I should tell Ely about my masters programme so that I could be given some respite to attend my lectures. But Rita advised me against that. I took her advice and continued to manage my time between the newsroom and the classroom.

But the clashes took a toll on my sanity. Ely had come to notice my occasional dashes in and out of office. Sometimes he would come over to my desk and notice that I was always reading books on Samuel Beckett. He always wondered why I was always reading Samuel Beckett. I was then writing my M.A Long Essay on the plays of Beckett. But the ultimate clash came on the day of the examination for the course. The examination held at the same time that the lecture normally held. I was in a fix. Very close to the time the examination was to start, I was still at TSM office in Ilupeju. But somehow, I stood up almost involuntarily, sauntered towards the exit door and made my way to Ikorodu road. Within minutes, I was aboard a taxi. By the time I got to campus, the examination was underway. I put in my best. At the end of the day, my performance in that course was neither good nor bad. It was average.

By November 1990, the examinations were over. I had only my Long Essay to grapple with. One month later, I concluded the programme. As it turned out, I was to leave TSM at the same time I concluded the Masters degree programme.

Just as I was stepping out of TSM, I was moving over to another News magazine called NEWSWAVE. There, I encountered a man called Mr. Ajulo. (I really didn't get to know his full names). The magazine was published by one Lawrence Okey Nnaji but Mr Ajulo, a fairly old man in his 60s then, was the head of editorial activities. He hailed from Modakeke in present-day Osun State and was always in the habit of telling stories about the Ife-Modakeke bloodletting.

I spent only four months at Newswave. But the bulk of my remembrances while at the magazine revolves around Mr. Ajulo.

I never really had any direct encounter with him. I concentrated on my beat and also joined in the production of the magazine. But little did I know that Mr. Ajulo did not like my carriage at all. He saw me as an arrogant young man who carried himself as if he was the only one that went to school. He harboured such impression about me silently. My presence irritated or suffocated him. But this was unknown to me. I respected him as a man who was old enough to be my father.

Then one day something happened. I hardly can remember what it was. What I can recall was that Mr. Ajulo blurted out. He lambasted me to my very face. He said I was always showing off. He said I was always talking as if I was the only one that had gone to obtain degrees. He said I was always choking and oppressing the atmosphere with my airs. He told me that he had a son studying at UNILAG. So, I should stop acting up since I was not the only one privileged to have attended UNILAG. When the man was done with his fury, I was too stupefied to utter any word. I did not understand the basis for the verbal assault. I considered it unprovoked. I looked at his age and decided to respect him. Mr. Nnaji, the publisher, was to intervene later. He consoled me. Mr. Ajulo had had his way. He had dressed me down. He probably felt triumphant that he had humbled the arrogant one.

But I did not hold the outburst against the old man. I dismissed it as one of those things that could happen in an office setting. I was to leave the magazine at the end of four months to join The Guardian Newspapers. That was in April 1991.

Chapter 4

STARTING A DOCTORATE

Before leaving NEWSWAVE Magazine at the end of March,1991, I had, a month earlier (February 1991), registered for my doctorate degree in English at the University of Lagos. My Masters degree result which was released in January 1991 was outstanding. I decided immediately the result was out to apply for the doctorate degree programme. I was admitted and subsequently employed by the university as a Graduate Assistant to teach Use of English. Consequently, I had to combine the doctorate programme, the teaching appointment and my career in Journalism at the same time.

The doctorate degree programme took off slowly but steadily. I spent a reasonable length of time modifying my research topic to suit what my supervisor, Dr (Mrs.) Karen King Aribisala (now a Professor of English) wanted. She has a bias for women writings and their feminist outlook. She got me to tailor my research interest in African-American Literature along that line. It should be noted that a research programme in African-American Literature was not my original preference. I had earlier opted to do my doctoral research in the area of Modern Drama. But there was no supervisor available to undertake the journey with me. Dr (Mrs) Ebun Clark, an authority in Dramatic Literature, was approached to supervise my doctorate degree programme. But she could not because she was going to retire in a few months time. I was advised not to start at all with her because her retirement could stall my doctorate programme unduly. Since the availability of a supervisor is one of the requirements that must be met before admission into the doctorate programme, I had to settle for African-American Literature where a supervisor was available.

By the time I enrolled for the doctorate degree programme, the Department of English of the University was still known for one thing. It had a notoriety for not producing Ph.D graduates. There were many cases of people who started the programme and abandoned it along the line. The impression the set-up created was that the Department was not keen on graduating her doctoral students. By the time I registered for the programme in February 1991, the Department had produced only three Ph.D graduates in its nearly 30 years of existence. Those of us who ventured into the programme at that time were therefore not too sure how we were going to end up. Regardless of this hang-up, I went into the programme with zeal and a determination to get to the Promised Land.

The way the programme ran in UNILAG then was that after formulating the conceptual and methodological framework for the research proposal , the candidate will make a presentation at a seminar at the Departmental level. Thereafter, he was expected to present his Pre-Dissertation findings at another Departmental seminar. When the two seminars have been successfully presented, the candidate's supervisor will then appear before a panel set up by the Post Graduate School to present the title of the candidate's thesis for approval. When the approval is secured, the candidate is then given the go-ahead to continue with his research work.

But something happened when my supervisor appeared before the panel at the Post Graduate School to present and defend the title of my thesis for approval. At the session, my supervisor, a West Indian married to a Nigerian, rejected and rebuffed the "inquisition" which some members of the panel subjected her to. She did not understand why people who hardly knew anything about Literature should be posing as experts. She called their bluff. With this development, some of the panelists concluded that she did not understand what my thesis was all about. The Post Graduate School therefore deferred the approval of the title of my thesis. Following the development, the Post Graduate School decided that candidates would, thenceforth, appear personally to defend the titles of their theses. The practice of having supervisors go for the defence was abolished.

The development at the Post Graduate School gave my department concern. The Departmental Post Graduate Committee had to schedule an emergency meeting to which I was invited. There, I was asked to make a presentation on my hypothesis to convince the Department once again (having done so twice during my seminar presentations) that my research was still on course. I did that brilliantly. I was asked to articulate my presentation and put same in writing. I did that and it was distributed to all the academic staff in the department for their consideration. Satisfied with my presentation, the department then wrote the Post Graduate School to say that candidate William Dr. Amanze Obi was ready to appear for the defence of the title of his thesis. I appeared before the Post Graduate School Panel subsequently and the title was approved without a whimper. I therefore became the first doctorate degree candidate at the University of Lagos to personally appear for the defence of the title of his thesis.

After four years of rigorous research work which saw me visiting the Whitney Young Library at the United States Information Service, Lagos to update myself on current issues in African-American Literature as well as female writings in America, my thesis was ready for submission to the Post Graduate School. On submission of the thesis, the school would constitute a panel of experts who would assess the thesis. The panelists were to be three. One was to come from my department. The other two were to be drawn from Departments of English of two other Nigerian universities.

My thesis was submitted to the then Acting Head of Department (HOD), Dr FBO Akporobaro, through my supervisor. The HOD was supposed to forward the thesis to the Departmental Post Graduate Committee which would in turn forward it to the Post Graduate School. But rather than do that, Dr Akporobaro sat on the thesis. Several months passed and no action was taken on my thesis. I became agitated. But my supervisor could not do much to assist. She was not the best of friends with Dr Akporobaro. Both did not get on well. She left me alone to carry my cross. It was at that time that I knew that Heads of Department were powerful in the University system. I was at the mercy of my HOD at that point in time. To get out of the situation, I complained to lecturers who were superior to the HOD but none of them could help me out. It was only Professor A.E. Eruvebetine of the department who was open enough to discuss the matter with me. He told me not to worry so much as that was part of the politics of Ph.D. He advised me not to mind the posturing from the HOD.

The HOD, on his part, was not interested in dealing with my supervisor in this matter. He preferred to deal with me directly. He would, from time to time, invite me over to his office and ask me to "lecture" him on my thesis. Each time I did that, he would remark thus: "Obi, you obviously know what you are doing. You have a good grasp of your research work. But my worry is that your supervisor does not seem to know what you are doing". I always chuckled at such a remark. It was uncharitable, to say the least. My supervisor was very much abreast of the issues that my thesis tackled. She was an expert in that field of study and could not have been ignorant of a work both of us went through together. She gave me a lot of reference materials on Women Studies which was an indication that she had carried out in-depth study in that area. But I did not take the HOD through all this. Rather, I would respond deferentially thus: "I am sure she knows what I am doing. After all, we went through this together. Maybe she has not discussed it with you". The man would then give me a deadpan look and ask me to go.

This went on for some months without progress. Then, the HOD decided to invent his own rule. He set up a panel of internal readers who went through my thesis and sent their comments to him. This was never the practice in the department. But Dr Akporobaro insisted on that. This rigmarole not withstanding, we still did not make progress. My thesis remained with him until his tenure expired. Prof Eruvbetine took over the headship of the department and within a few weeks of his assumption of office, my thesis left the department for the Post Graduate School. A panel of experts comprising Dr Akachi Ezeigbo (now a Professor of English) as Internal Reader and Professors Ebele Eko and Helen Chukwuma of the Department of English of the Universities of Calabar and Port Harcourt respectively. They returned favourable verdicts on the thesis.

Dr. Ezeigbo's Report was as follows:

1. A clear and detailed evaluation of the Thesis
    i. Originality of the work: The thesis is original and provides fresh and profound insights into the works of Toni Morrison and Alice Walker.
    ii. Evidence of Competence in the Field of Study: The study reveals not only the candidate's competent examination of the themes highlighted in the novels but also a remarkable analysis of the various aspects of the novelist's styles and techniques.

iii. Assessment of critical judgment of the thesis: Please itemize:
   1. The thesis shows that Morrison and Walker have indeed re-defined and re-imaged the African-American female in their novels.
   2. Mr. Obi's adoption of the historical, feminist and formalist approaches to criticism in his analysis has enabled him to show how the novels studied contributed to a deeper understanding of male-female relationships as well as the predicament of the African-American women which is a result of sexism and racism.
iv. Worth of material in the Thesis for purposes of publication:
   I would expect much of the thesis to be publishable. The study is well-researched and the candidate's scholarship is not in doubt. His reading is as wide as can be expected.
v. Its contributions to knowledge, Please itemize:
   1. Morrison and Walker's treatment of the themes of sexism, racism and struggle in the life of the African-American women is given clarity and fresh insights.
   2. The thesis competently analyses the remarkable developments in the styles and techniques of the two novelists as they explore the experiences of black women.
vi. Satisfactoriness as regards literary presentation:
   The thesis is very readable and is written in straightforward and lucid style. Mr. Obi has a generally good style. There are hardly any errors. The chapters are properly linked and the goals clearly stated. Clarity is the word!
2. An unequivocal declaration as to the adequacy or otherwise of the Thesis for the Ph.D. degree

I believe that the candidate has handled his subject properly both in content and in presentation for the thesis to be accepted for the Ph.D. degree.

That was Dr Ezigbo's approving remarks on my research work. Prof. Ebele Eko's was to follow. Her Report read as follows:

1. A clear and detailed evaluation of the Thesis:
    i. Originality of the work: He has made judicious use of secondary materials. On the whole, the work is original.
    ii. Evidence of competence in the field of study: There is clear evidence that he grasped and effectively articulated the ideological and aesthetic complexities of two complex writers: Morrison and Walker. It flows.
    iii. Assessment of critical judgment of the thesis: Please itemize:
        1. Grapples intelligently with the ramifications of language in the feminist discourse.
        2. Lucid and insightful explication of texts.
        3. Sustained argument.
        4. Focus on topic and perceptive criticism.
        5. Evidence of wide reading and acknowledgement of sources.
    iv. Worth of material in the thesis for purposes of publication:
        This work is very fertile with publication potentials. Journal articles can easily emerge. Two books on the two authors or one comparative work. The thesis is rich.
    v. Its contributions to knowledge: Please itemize:
        1. Very good literature review and abstract.
        2. Fairly detailed study on all the novels of Morrison and Walker.
        3. Good criticism, especially on language.

4. Significant addition to the study of sexism, racism, feminism and womanism. An important contribution indeed.

vi. Satisfactoriness as regards literary presentation:
Literary presentation is very good, however, the documentation is pre-1984. The new MLA style of documentation must be adopted for this 1996 work. Excellent proof reading.

2. An unequivocal declaration as to the adequacy or otherwise of the Thesis for the Ph.D degree
I strongly recommend this thesis for a Ph.D degree (subject to documentation adjustments and very minor corrections).

That was Prof. Ebele Eko's unequivocal endorsement of my thesis.

With that process completed, a Panel of Examiners was subsequently set up for the final assessment of the thesis. I appeared before the panel on March 4, 1997 and successfully defended the thesis. The degree of Doctor of Philosophy (Ph.D) was then awarded to me.

In May of the same year, the university held the convocation ceremony for graduands of the 1995/1996 session. I was chosen as the Valedictorian for the convocation.

That effectively marked the end of my doctorate degree programme at the University of Lagos. It also saw me leaving the university system completely to pay more attention to the journalism profession.

Part Two
The Newspaper Years

Chapter 5

FROM THE GUARDIAN TO THISDAY

My years as a doctorate degree student ran side by side with the period I worked with The Guardian newspapers. While I registered for the doctorate degree programme in February 1991, I assumed duties at the Newspaper house in April of the same year. Significantly, I ended my career at The Guardian at the time I was through with my Ph.D work.

My engagement by The Guardian came by chance. I did not really go to the Newspaper house in search of employment. I had visited Rutam House (the newspaper's corporate headquarters) early in 1991 to pay homage and respect to a good-natured gentleman, Ben Tomoloju, who was the Arts Editor of the newspaper at that time. My literary contributions to the newspaper while I was an undergraduate and during my NYSC days were published by Mr. Tomoloju. When I returned to Lagos after the NYSC scheme, I was literally consumed by the engagements that came my way, particularly the Masters degree programme. More than one year passed before I could realize that I had not been in touch with Mr Tomoloju. So, on this particular day, I strolled into The Guardian Newsroom and met BT, as he was popularly called. He screamed when he saw me."Where have you been?"he asked excitedly, holding my hands. After exchanging pleasantries,

I reviewed my movements and engagements with him. As a fresh graduate who was yet to get a job, it was taken for granted that I needed one even though I was engaged in full-time post graduate studies. Consequently, BT remarked that my style of writing would be suitable for the weekend titles of the newspaper. There and then, he asked me to see the then Editor of The Guardian on Sunday, Mr Emeka Izeze. On meeting with Mr Izeze, he referred me further to the Magazine Desk of the Sunday newspaper edited by Obasi Ogbonnaya. When I got there, I was to discover that my long-standing friend and a kindred spirit with a degree in English from the University of Ife (now Obafemi Awolowo University), John Odey Aduma, was already working at the Magazine Desk. John was excited to see me. He said I should just come and join them so that, together, we would be churning out literary masterpieces for the newspaper.

Ben Tomoloju and John Aduma knew me well and could swear by Jove that I was a brilliant writer. But the practice at The Guardian then was that a potential employee must be tested. In order to determine my writing strength , Obasi dispatched me immediately to Idumota on the Lagos Island. The sprawling market territory was witnessing some skirmishes on that very day. Obasi asked me to go there, observe and report the incident. I did as instructed and returned the next day with my report. The story was arresting. In it, I brought my descriptive abilities into sharp focus. The presentation was almost cinematic. Obasi was in love with it. It was a clincher. With it, I had a job waiting for me at the newspaper house. I returned to my place of work at NEWSWAVE and continued with my financial reporting. But unknown to me, The Guardian had prepared my appointment letter, waiting for me to come and take up the job of a Staff Reporter. I returned to the Newsroom weeks later without knowing that my letter of appointment had been waiting for me.

That was how the journey at The Guardian began. While at the Sunday Newspaper, I travelled extensively across the country to report stories for the newspaper. I visited over 20 out of the then 30 States of the Federation in the course of my assignments. The experience was both exciting and challenging. I embraced both. Today, I owe my good knowledge of the Nigerian geography largely to the trips I made for The Guardian.

I was later to be transferred to the News Desk of the Sunday newspaper. This was during the ascension of Kingsley Osadolor as the Editor of The Guardian on Sunday. It was while on the News Desk that I became a foreign affairs analyst, in addition to the other assignments that I undertook at the Newspaper.

At The Guardian at that time, Osadolor cut the image of a bully especially as the Deputy Editor of the newspaper. He yelled and shouted at Reporters who were slow and sluggish in meeting deadlines. But I got on very well with him while he was the Editor of The Guardian on Sunday. His first encounter with me was through my story. I had, sometime in 1992, travelled to Okomu Wildlife Sanctuary (now Okomu National Park) in Edo State to do a story for the newspaper. On my return, I wrote the story and sent it to my editor without a byline. When the story got to Kingsley, he used his red ink on it. He had asked, "Who wrote this story?" I was eventually identified as the writer. Kingsley had nice words for me. In fact, as my editor, Osadolor was in the habit of giving me kudos for my stories. But sometimes after praising me, he would turn around to reprimand himself thus: "Why am I even praising you for doing your job?" Each time he said this, both of us would laugh and thereafter move on to other issues. Looking back, I consider Osadolor as the best boss that I ever had.

Chapter 6

THE INTERREGNUM

By 1994, my stay at The Guardian was rudely punctuated by the unwarranted closure of the newspaper house by the repressive military regime of the time. The then Head of State, General Sani Abacha, had in August of that year proscribed The Guardian alongside Concord and The Punch Newspapers. Consequently, Rutam House, the headquarters of The Guardian titles, came under lock and key. The absence of The Guardian, The Punch and Concord newspapers created a huge vacuum in the print media space in Nigeria. The situation presented an opportunity for some investors to try their hands on publishing. Fortuitously, a few newspapers came aboard the turbulent scene in a bid to fill the gap.

But The Guardian took steps to ensure that its ranks were not badly depleted by the emerging newspapers, regardless of its closure. To achieve this objective, the Management of The Guardian decided to retain those members of staff that it regarded as "swift hands". Whereas every other member of staff was asked to go home without salary pending when the newspaper would be de-proscribed, the swift hands were relocated to another property of the Ibrus in Iganmu and placed on half salary as a form of motivation.

I was among the swift hands retained by the newspaper. We met fairly regularly then to discuss and write stories. The stories were kept in a story-bank and were expected to serve as a buffer whenever the newspaper house was reopened. I kept faith with the arrangement for six months. But there was intense pressure from some quarters for me to join a new publication. Eventually, some serious poachers came in the name of Third Eye Newspapers, based in Ibadan. They came with an enticing offer. At the end of the day, they succeeded in attracting a good number of us from The Guardian. The new team which came mainly from The Guardian congregated at Ibadan and, together, we pioneered Third Eye newspapers.

The movement to Ibadan posed a great challenge to me. At that time, I was still involved in my triple engagements, namely, my Ph.D programme, my teaching job at the university and my newspaper job. My commitment as teacher and researcher required my regular presence on campus. The result was that I shuttled Ibadan and Lagos very frequently, averaging three times a week. I needed to cover both flanks properly and I did that to the best of my abilities.

With the experience and expertise of those of us who came from The Guardian, Third Eye took off on a sound note. It continued to show signs of promise months after its debut. But trouble started when the financiers of the Newspaper could no longer keep their own side of the bargain. They could not sustain the attractive salary they offered us. In the fifth month, the newspaper had begun to owe members of staff. This was followed up shortly after with a 50 percent slash in staff salaries. For those of us from Lagos, we knew that it was time to return to base. Luckily, by the sixth month of our employment at Third Eye, The Guardian was reopened and those of us who left for Ibadan returned in droves to Lagos. That was in September 1995.

On resumption at The Guardian, I continued with my foreign affairs analyses, among other topical assignments for the newspaper.

The Interregnum

In less than one year from then, my foreign commentaries had become very well received in diplomatic circles. It commanded attention among the readership and I received tremendous kudos for my insightful analyses. My fame had preceded me and many wanted to get to know me.

By that time, I had completed my doctorate degree programme. What was left was my viva. With my enhanced academic status, I felt that I needed a bigger challenge. I wanted to be more meaningfully engaged. THISDAY, one of the Newspapers that emerged during the proscription, had advertised for the position of Editorial Page Editor. The newspaper needed a high profile individual to fill the position. I applied for the job. But the position eventually went to Dr Bola A. Akinterinwa who was then a Senior Research Fellow at the Nigerian Institute of International Affairs. He spent his sabbatical leave on the job.

However, a few months later, I got a message from Mr. Victor Ifijeh who had become the Editor of THISDAY. He said he was in love with my foreign affairs analyses and wanted me to be the newspaper's Foreign Affairs Editor. Victor collected my Curriculum Vitae and penned his recommendation on it to Okagbue Aduba who was then the General Manager of the newspaper. Okagbue was to make recommendation to the Chairman/Editor-in-Chief, Nduka Obaigbena, for his approval. However, for reasons that were best known to him, Okagbue withheld his recommendation. After waiting fruitlessly for a few weeks for Okagbue's endorsement, Victor decided that we should go and see Mr. Obaigbena directly. As we made to climb upstairs, we ran into the man on the staircase. Victor told him my name and it quickly caught his attention. "Did you apply for the position of Editorial Page Editor when we advertised?" he asked. I said yes. He immediately grabbed one of my hands and practically dragged me to his office. He checked the records and confirmed that I was one of those who sat for the competency test for the position of Editorial Page Editor. He then asked Victor to produce my Curriculum Vitae for the position of Foreign Affairs Editor. Victor told him that it was with Okagbue. He summoned the man immediately. "Where is this man's CV?" he hollered. Okagbue muttered some incomprehensible things. Obaigbena ordered him to produce it. Okagbue dashed to his office and came back with it. "Why have you not minuted on it?" Obaigbena queried. Okagbue had no answer. Obaigbena then ordered him to sign. He did that and he (Obaigbena) approved. It was instantaneous. There was no stalking. There was no hang-up.

I returned to The Guardian that day and began the process of my disengagement. I eventually left the newspaper at the end of September 1996 and was signed on at THISDAY on October 1, 1996 as Foreign Affairs Editor.

I had a rapid career progression at THISDAY Newspapers. Obaigbena, a liberal employer, always gave the Journalists in the stable of his newspapers the opportunity to grow. Shortly after my assumption of office as Foreign Affairs Editor of THISDAY, I went for the defence of my thesis. With a Ph.D in my kitty, my perception of what I should be doing in a newspaper house changed. It was, and still is, unusual for a Ph.D holder to be seen in the newsroom. It is odd through and through. That is why it is extremely difficult for a doctorate degree holder to go through the mills of journalism practice. The few that find themselves in newspaper houses usually take refuge in the Editorial Board. It was in the light of this reality that the pull between the classroom and the newsroom began for me. One of my Lecturers at the University of Lagos, Dr E.A Babalola (now late), always encouraged me to join the academic staff of the university. He believed that it is in imparting knowledge that one can realise the full potentials of his academic training. In fact, he had no respect for newspaper articles. He always said to me then, "Great Obi, you know these things you people write in newspapers are not serious things". He always said this amid peals of laughter. His recommendation was that I should remain with the university system.

However, because I had spent a reasonable number of years already as a newspaper man before acquiring my Ph.D, I was not too persuaded to leave the profession. At best, I said that I would take my career in journalism to a logical conclusion and then move over to the classroom. But the urge to remain a part of the university community was still there. I was practically caught between two stools.

Given this clash of interest, I was, as a Ph.D holder, no longer too keen in the nitty gritty of the newspaper business. I felt that the Editorial Board may just be manageable for me as an intellectual. I told Obaigbena my preference and he took note of it. In spite of this, I continued to function in my capacity as Foreign Affairs Editor until the time the Chairman, Obaigbena, considered it necessary to challenge me with another responsibility.

Chapter 7

VOYAGE TO CONGO

The high point of my tenure as the Foreign Affairs Editor was my visit, in the company of Dr Bola Akinterinwa, to Kinshasa, capital city of the Democratic Republic of Congo in September 1997. Kinshasa, sprawling seemingly forever from the banks of the Congo River, gave us ample room for exploration. But we were focused on a major political assignment. Then, Laurent Kabila, the country's Head of State, had a few months earlier, staged a coup that brought him to power. The country was sitting on edge on account of the forceful take-over of the government. But Kabila had a blueprint for the Congo of his dream.

As the foreign editor of the newspaper and an analyst of note, I ran a number of analyses on the development in the Congo. But Mr. Obaigbena who cherishes excellence a lot, wanted more. It was that predilection of his that always gave THISDAY an edge over other newspapers at that time. It was for this reason that he dispatched me to the Congo to cover and report the affairs of the new government in the country. Dr. Akinterinwa was asked to join me since he could speak French, the official language of country. ,We spent 10 days in Kin, as the locals romantically refer to Kinshasa, where we had extensive interaction with senior members of the government of Kabila. By the time we returned, we had become very knowledgeable in the affairs of the Congo.

My report in THISDAY of October 5, 1997, said it all. It reads in part.

"A few weeks to May 17, 1997, the signs were there that the apple carte was in danger of being upstaged. But because President Mobutu Sese Seko of the Republic of Zaire had, in the past, warded off rebellious skirmishes such as the one being led then by a dark horse called Laurent Desire Kabila, it was hardly necessary to jump unto the victory bandwagon. To have done so would have been impolitic given Mobutu's more than 30-year grip on the Republic.

"In the light of this, Laurent Kabila's armed insurrection against the government of a man whose name was synonymous with conquest, was at best, seen as a tolerable menace that would be taken care of at the appropriate time. But because the germs of the revolution that eventually threw Mobutu overboard had vegetated to fruition, what was thought to be mere rebellious bravado eventuated into a full blown armed confrontation. Within seven months into the revolutionary struggle, President Mobutu went with the winds. Laurent Kabila was ably recognized by the United States of America, which had investments to protect in Kinshasa. The result was the soft-landing which the revolutionaries made in Kinshasa.

"But the revolution of May 17 was no mere happenstance. It was no coincidence either. It was a well-worn action plan backed by a clearly articulated revolutionary blueprint. The dream was long in coming to fruition. For so many years, the idea enjoyed the uncertainty of purgatory. No one was sure of whether the idea would berth on a safe harbour. When it eventually did, Laurent Kabila who led the revolution that saw most of the actors gravitating into insanity in exile in Europe and Africa went for the blueprint. The result is an assemblage of cultured nationalists whose vision for the new Congo is unwavering in commitment and sophistication.

"Today, the Democratic Republic of Congo is peopled and manned by these militant members of the African socialist revolution. As idealists, they had a dream. As men who believe in practicality, they strove to give meaning and urgency to their cause. With verve, they defended their vision of what the Congo should be. In this vein, they had to collapse their omnibus ideology into a form that is wieldy. The Kabila government as is presently constituted is directed by these men of vision.

"At the head of these revolutionaries who together with Kabila are insisting on injecting a fresh impetus into the socio-economic and political life of the Congolese, is a man called Pierre Victor Mpoyo. He is perhaps, one of the earliest of Congolese who saw through the smokescreen that Mobutu erected shortly after seizing the reins of governance from Patrice Lumumba and Joseph Kasavubu. Mpoyo is the Minister of Economy, Commerce and Industry under the new dispensation.

"In 1966, just one year into Mobutu's misrule in the Congo, Mpoyo had cause to identify with the government of Mobutu. Apparently fascinated by the nationalistic dreams which Mpoyo paraded, Mobutu said of him: He is "a worthy and devoted son of Congo, who everywhere and continuously will support it in its Africanity". Mobutu was right. He was much more so, since he himself made pretenses then to Africanity. Perhaps one way in which Mobutu demonstrated his pan-Africanist pretensions was in his quixotic displacement of European influences in the Congo in the early 1970s. But because the likes of Mpoyo could see through the wall of deceit erected by Mobutu, his balloon stood the danger of busting. Alienation came in 1973 when Mobutu, on his return from China declared before 100,000 people that: "God does not exist; if he did, He could not condemn 800 million Chinese who do not believe in him." With this declaration, Mpoyo said he lost respect for Mobutu. Their relationship soured and because

Mobutu was ruthless with opposition elements, Mpoyo went on exile.

"At 62, Mpoyo does not look or sound tired. His socialist ideals are still intact. In an interview with THISDAY about a fortnight ago, he enthused: "I never change. I am the same. My socialism is for all, not for a few". From the ministry of economy where Mpoyo sits, he has lofty ideals for the Congo, especially as it concerns post-war reconstruction. While Mobutu's reign lasted, Mpoyo's major regret was that there was no democracy in the Congo. It was on the basis of this that he rebelled against Mobutu. For so many years, they plotted his ouster. For so many years they failed.

While recounting his role in the overthrow of Mobutu, Mpoyo said: "We tried, failed; we tried again and again until we succeeded". While all this lasted, Mpoyo shared the ideals of western liberalism founded on multi-party democracy. He was in love with the policy and wanted it for the Congo. From his base in the east of the Congo, Mpoyo's dream was that democracy and liberalism would soon flower in his fatherland.

"He returned to the Congo on June 27, 1997 to see to the realization of his pet project. But because democracy can hardly thrive in an economy that is badly battered, Mpoyo says the Kabila government would put democracy on hold for three years. He assured, however, that Congo would embrace democracy. "We will definitely go to election. We fought for so many years for democracy. So we must have democracy. We definitely have a democratic agenda. But we want to rebuild the country first. There are no roads, no telecommunication system, no infrastructure. So we must revamp the economy first. It is for this reason that Mr. Etienne Tshisekedi, four – time prime minister and frontline politician, may not work together with the Kabila administration. According to Mpoyo, Tshisekedi wants immediate return to politics at a time the economy is in dire straits. "I invited him to join my ministry. But he was talking politics. If he wants politics, then he must see the other imaginations except to become prime minister. If he joins in rebuilding the economy, we can go to election together. Under Mobutu, he was busy battling for supremacy. But today, we are under emergency". Mpoyo said.

"Under the present arrangement, the Kabila government has a three-year transition programme. According to Mpoyo, all structures will be put in place by three years, within which period elections could hold. "We want people to regain their dignity by the end of the transition", he declared. This, he said, is a commitment the Kabila government has made to the people of Congo. "We don't have to tell the international community. The big powers are not our master. Our people, we respect them. And we made the commitment to them".

"As one who worked together with Kabila, Mpoyo said he has no doubt that both of them were working for the upliftment of the people of Congo. While Kabila was the leader of the Alliance of Democratic Forces for the Liberation of Congo (AFDL), Mpoyo was its spokesman in exile. And because he does not change, President Kabila believes religiously in his doggedness and commitment to the cause for which Mobutu was overthrown. "There is no difference of opinion between the president and I. We never split. We think the same way. We have the same commitment, on economy, on social programmes like income tax. Together we are putting up a social programme. We are also planning for free education and free health". Mpoyo said.

"These are national reconstruction programmes which demand astuteness and expertise. In order to ensure that the ship of state is properly piloted in this regard, the Kabila administration created a ministry for National Reconstruction and Emergencies. It is presided over by a technocrat called Mr. Etienne Richard Mbaya. Since he assumed office as the National Reconstruction Minister,

Mr. Mbaya has been saddled with a number of reconstruction programmes. In fact, his ministry has concluded arrangements to organize a National Conference on Reconstruction (CNR). According to the Minister, the conference on Reconstruction is being planned as an offshoot of the mobilization and participation agenda unfolded by President Kabila in his address to the people of Congo on June 30, 1997. But if president Kabila's projection three years ago was a dream, Mr. Mbaya said it was time to translate it into reality. According to Mbaya, the agenda is a Congolese movement of the Congolese people in their resolve to combine their efforts, intelligence and know-how for national development. As a collective effort, the conference will bring together artisans, workers, employees of the commercial sector, and intellectuals in research, schools, universities and civil servants among others. To realize this objective, the conference, Mbaya said, will have two main components.

"The first component which he described as the first stage will take place in all the provinces and Kinshasa, and will comprise the representatives of the different rural and urban communities. Its objective will be to assess the situation in areas concerned and define their needs in the area of reconstruction. 25 delegates will be elected from among the participants. The provincial conference will take place from November 17 to 22, 1997. The second stage will focus on the main event of the National Conference on Reconstruction and will be held in Kinshasa from December 8 to 20, 1997. It will comprise the delegates from the hinterland. According to Mbaya, a permanent secretariat will be put in place for the preparation and organization of the conference. The aim of the exercise, according to Mbaya, is to put in place a National Commission for the definition of a national reconstruction programme. It will also put in place the means of reconstruction such as social and economic council at the national and local levels, a bank for reconstruction and development and provincial companies for development.

"Prior to the idea of the National Conference on Reconstruction, a sovereign national conference and a colloquium of development priorities were held in the country. Mbaya regretted that the efforts did not produce desired results. The National Conference on Reconstruction then, Mbaya said, seeks to be an instrument for the actualization and concretization of the aspirations of the Congolese people, with the assistance of the masses.

"The Sovereign National Conference described as a colossal failure by the Kabila administration was the brainchild of the Mobutu Government. In the last days of the administration, Mobutu constantly sought for ways and means to remain relevant. Consequently, he organized a Sovereign National Conference, which unfortunately resolved nothing. The conference was a government project and largely sought to address matters that were of interest to the Mobutu regime. In it, the opposition was not given a free hand although the impression given was that the conference was open and national. Because it believed that the conference under Mobutu was a deceit, Kabila's government sought to counter it soon after it came to power. To this end, it held a colloquium in July 1997. But as pointed out by Mbaya, the colloquium did not make any significant impact on the people because it was elite-based. It was a forum of experts, who were mandated by the new government in Congo to analyze the priorities of government in the area of implementation of a Triennial plan. The National Conference on Reconstruction, Mbaya said, avoids this approach. Its focus is on the grassroots, who would be mobilized to define their own priorities. He described the grassroots as the motor, the actors and beneficiaries of the development plan.

"As part of its efforts to give the revolution a bite, the Kabila government is dismantling old structures and erecting new ones. To achieve this objective, a redefinition of government's international cooperation pacts is in the offing. This is especially tailored to embrace countries which were harsh to Mobutu in his last days. A little over a week ago, a Belgian Economic mission visited Kinshasa to join the Kabila government in evolving an economic agenda that would turn things around for the better. Before now, programmes which were ostensibly development-oriented were placed squarely and roundly on the altar of politics. But because the Kabila administration believes strongly that a development agenda which will achieve the goals of the revolution must be insulated from petty interests, it has placed at the helm technocrats who can sift the grain from the chaff. Consequently, a ministry for international cooperation has been created under the leadership of Professor Thomas Kanzas.

"Having taken a close and hard look at the mentality that ruled the economy and, in fact, the entire polity before the advent of the revolutionaries, Professor Kanzas believes that one way out of the quagmire would be a change in the mentality of the people. In this regard, he advocates the separation of politics from economic cooperation. For Kanzas, Belgo-Congolese relationship goes beyond that of marriage. According to him, Belgium is married to Europe but is unavoidably in love with Congo. He, therefore, believes that an economic Marshall Plan for Congo based on a mutual relationship with Belgium was imperative.

"Mr. Etienne Mbaga, the Minister for National Reconstruction and Emergencies, was even more pointed. According to him, the Congo of today is anchored on the philosophy of economic cooperation. But that is not to say that Congo has no policy thrust. According to Mbaga, assistance from international cooperation will be guided by three principles. There is going to be delimitation of operation for each foreign partner. This involves the identification of a geo-political area in each province or well defined operational zone. The second principle will involve the orientation of foreign partners towards well determined sectors where they can contribute better to national reconstruction programmes. And there is, lastly, government's wish and desire that foreign partners should give the same Marshall Plan of support given by the United States to Europe. The Belgian delegation was the first from Western Europe to visit Congo since Kabila took over the reins of governance. In this regard, Mr. Mbaya pointed out that a new page in Belgo-Congolese cooperation has been turned and that this would pave way for a new era of hope and active solidarity.

"But for Mr. Oscar Mudiay Wa Mudiay, the Director of Cabinet in the Ministry of Economy and Commerce, time has come to renegotiate the legal basis of Congo's relationship with Belgium. The relationship, before now, is guided by the convention of January 24, 1969 relating to the promotion of trade and Lome IV Convention. Belgium as it is today, accounts for about 21.8 per cent of total Congolese import. It also remains the first supplier to Congo, coming before South Africa and the United States. Belgium is also the first client of Congo. Balance of trade between both countries, since 1993, has been to the advantage of Congo.

"Notwithstanding, the Congolese economy has been fraught with hiccups. There is the general decline in the Gross Domestic Product (GDP), suspension of direct economic cooperation with Congo by hostile countries, non-diversification and the inability of Congolese products to compete favourably with their counterparts elsewhere, and more. In the face of these difficulties, Congo is advocating the intensification of efforts and increased trade missions as well as stronger cooperation between public and private trade organizations. According to Mudiay, "Our partnership should no longer be represented by this regrettable image which sees raw materials exported to Europe for transformation to finished manufactured goods and then later resold to the Southern hemisphere at exorbitant prices". He called for a soft and more humane image which will make Belgian enterprises to focus on industrialization and transformation of raw materials in Congo. As he puts it. "The protection of persons and goods is the epistle of the new Congo".

"The revolutionary programme is, indeed, encompassing. Apart from seeking economic cooperation, the work force is also being streamlined to avoid the wastage and patronages of the Mobutu era. This is one area in which the government is nearly on collision course with the workers. Although the revolutionary agenda is supposed to be populist, workers who were being owed arrears of salaries during the time of Mobutu are expecting that the new government would settle the arrears of salaries being owed them. During Mobutu, ghost workers almost made the economy prostrate. This state of affairs is what government wants to avoid.

"Explaining government's stance on this, Mr. Oscar Mudiay of the Ministry of Economy told THISDAY that government does not want to run government by patronage as was the case with Mobutu. According to him, the Kabila government met an empty treasury and therefore is embarking on aggressive cost-saving measures to reduce government expenditure to the barest minimum. To achieve this objective, he said government does not want to rush into paying unproductive, redundant and ghost workers.

"Perhaps, one area which the revolution is bound to affect is the diplomatic circle. Given the hostility of part of the international community, the Kabila government appears poised to take on the international community. And this has to be achieved through trained and qualified diplomats. Right now, Kabila's government believes it has no diplomats abroad. Plans are therefore underway to recall them. According to Mr. Mpoyo, the Congolese government is to train ambassadors who would then be appointed and assigned to countries. Interested diplomats among the serving are free to participate. They would be sent abroad for the training programme. The aim is to give the diplomats the right kind of orientation.

"Beyond these, the Kabila administration looks set to turn the table in its favour. The frenzy and flurry of activities in government establishments are clear pointers to the determination of the government to revolutionize not only the Democratic Republic of Congo but also the entire Central African sub region."[11]

Chapter 8

A REVOLUTION UNDER THREAT

The report in the last chapter captured the situation in the Congo Democratic Republic in the last quarter of 1997. However, regardless of the laudable and revolutionary blueprint which President Laurent Kabila and his team of experts outlined, the situation in Congo at that time was not a rose without thorns. The major obstacles which the government had to contend with were the crisis in the eastern part of the country, the United Nations (UN) fact-finding team and the Congolese press. They were the sore points of Kabila's march towards a brand new nation.

Although the war in eastern Congo was an inter tribal affair, President Kabila, according to his lieutenants, was deeply worried by it. And this was hardly surprising. For a man who assumed the reins of governance through armed insurrection, skirmishes such as the one in eastern Congo was bound to bother him. This was especially so in the light of the fact that his government was yet to stand on a firm footing. That explained why he did not sit askance in the hope that the problem would take care of itself. He was involved, and he offered the olive branch through overtures and manoeuvres.

The United Nations was a different ball game. There was, at that time, a UN fact-finding team in Kinshasa. The team arrived the country on August 24, 1997. Its mission was to investigate the alleged massacre of Rwandan Hutus by Kabila's rebel group, the Alliance of Democratic Forces for Liberation of Congo (AFDL) when it was on the rampage in the bid to liberate Zaire from the 32-year grip of Mobutu Sese Seko.

Mr. Pierre-Victor Mpoyo, the strongman of President Kabila's government then, decried the activities of the UN team in Congo, describing it as irresponsible. He said the team, on arrival, carried on in a manner that was intended to provoke the Kabila administration. In the words of Mpoyo, "those gentlemen have been here for some time. Before coming, they were supposed to dispatch a message to us so that a proper arrangement could be made to welcome them. But they did not do this. They arrived without notice". According to Mpoyo, the government was completely taken unawares. They came when officials of the Kabila government were traveling to South Africa. "We were going on a cooperation visit to South Africa when we heard that the UN team is here", he said.

Nevertheless, Mr. Mpoyo said government tried to accommodate and welcome them. To this end, Mr. Etienne Mbaya of the Ministry of Reconstruction, was mandated to receive them. "He met with them, tried to help them and make arrangements to visit the eastern part of the country where their mission was supposed to be", Mpoyo said. But Mpoyo was worried that despite all the assistance and courtesies extended to them by the Kabila administration, the team members were yet to start work. And that was in September, one month after their arrival in the country. Rather, they were still in Kinshasa trying to find mass graves where the Rwandan refugees were said to have been buried. He said the team members were apparently not enthusiastic about the work they were sent to do. "They don't appear to be in a hurry probably because of the allowance of $2,000.00 (two thousand dollars) which a member is entitled to per day", he noted.

Disputing the UN team's claim of mass massacre of refugees, he said those killed were no refugees, they were armed. They were former military men defeated and chased out by the Rwandan government. They were helped to enter Congo by French troops. They crossed the border with military equipment and Mobutu let them in. According to him, the Democratic Republic of Congo was not a forest where somebody could go to and wander about. It is a country governed by rules and regulations. To this end, he said the UN team members would be asked out of the country as soon as their visas expired. As far as the Kabila government was concerned, the UN team led by a Togolese diplomat, Mr. Atsu-Kofi Amega, was biased against the Congolese government. To avoid a situation where the team would wilfully pass a verdict of guilt on the Congolese government, Kabila had to ask that the Organization of African Unity (OAU) be involved in the fact-finding mission. According to Mr. Mpoyo, the then OAU chairman, Mr. Robert Mugabe, was already well disposed to the idea of an OAU involvement. An OAU involvement, he also said, would guard against manipulation. "Right now, they are taking pictures, interviewing people, we don't want that", he said. According to him also, the UN team's insistence that it would go to Mbandaka which lies on the west of the country was an act of provocation. "Their mandate does not cover that. It is a breach of the protocol agreement", he said.

But the UN team would not accept an OAU involvement. According to the team, the mission as constituted, cannot work together with the OAU. Mr. Jose Diaz, the spokesman of the UN team in the Democratic Republic of Congo, said there was an independent team set up by the Secretary-General of the UN. "Unless the team is reconstituted, it cannot collaborate with the OAU", he said. It cannot also be monitored by government agents as demanded by Kabila government. According to him, government can only provide facilitators like forensic experts or security men. It cannot have members who will listen to the team's interview with people or monitor the exhumation of bodies or autopsy work on them.

The Congolese government had as one of its conditions to the team demanded an OAU involvement and a provision by the UN of 1.7 million dollars as allowance to government's agents who would join the UN team in its investigation. Mr. Diaz said, however, that the team was not thinking of meeting those demands. "There is no provision for the 1.7 million dollars. The question is being discussed at political level between the Secretary-General and Kabila", he said. Again, he insisted that the work of the team cannot be overseen by external bodies- be they OAU or government members. He said this was unnecessary since the team was committed to impartiality.

The team was also unimpressed by government's charge of bias on the team leader, Mr. Atsu Kofi Amega, a Togolese, due to his home government's support for the ousted Mobutu administration. The team said the charge of partiality was uncalled for since Amega was an international civil servant whose allegiance was to the UN rather than to his home government. According to Diaz, the team was obliged to be impartial and neutral. "We are international civil servants. It is in our oath of office. We don't work for sectional interests. The fact that the Congolese government accepted our mission means they believe we can be impartial and neutral, at least in principle". Diaz also held that Mr. Amega was chosen because of his wealth of experience, having done the work before. He was also known for his objectivity. Arguing further, the UN spokesman said Kabila's government had no reason to suspect Amega since his leadership of the team was known and communicated to the government before their arrival. "There was no objection. The first time we heard of objection was on August 27, 1997, three days after our arrival in Kinshasa", he pointed out.

Because of the many areas of disagreement between government and the UN team, the mission was in a state of inactivity for a reasonable period of time while waiting for directives from the UN headquarters in Geneva. The team was supposed to complete its work by December 31, 1997.

As the government grappled with all this, the Congolese Press was another headache which it had to contend with. For instance, on Thursday, September 18, 1997, all newspapers in the country went off the newsstands in protest against the arrest, detention and harassment of journalists. A specific instance was the arrest and detention of Mr. Muboyayi Mubanga, the Editor of Le Phane.

Worried by what it called undue harassment of its members, an organization called Media Libre, Media Pour Tours (Free Media, Media For All) called its members to action. Apart from the no-newspaper day, the organization said it would embark on a peaceful demonstration with masked faces if its grievances were not addressed.

At a press conference which had its theme as "Press, Democracy and Congo in Peril," Mr. Andre Abeiye Mobiko, the secretary of Media Libre who was also the Editor-in-Chief of La Reference said Congo was imperiled due to the absence of a free press. He said democracy would not thrive in an atmosphere where there is no free press.

However, in spite of all this, the Congolese government did not believe that it was muzzling the press. Mr. Mpoyo held then that the Press in Congo was free. "But we expect them to be responsible. They can help to mobilize the people and rebuild the country. They should help to promote the economy rather than embark on strikes and observe no-working day. It is ridiculous", Mpoyo said.

According to him, Congo at that time was bankrupt. What was needed then was rebuilding it, not politicking.

This was the state of affairs with the Congo that we visited. We returned with first-hand information about the goings-on in the country. The stories that emanated from the trip gave THISDAY another mileage. It placed it above its competitors in the Nigerian newspaper market.

After a fulfilling tenure as Foreign Affairs Editor of THISDAY, the Chairman/Editor-in-Chief felt that it was time for me to move on. That was how I got redeployed to the Editorial Board as Deputy Editorial Page Editor. Akinterinwa and I ran the Board for more than one year. Then an idea came to the chairman again. He invited me over to his office and told me what he wanted to do. He wanted me to return to the newsroom as Deputy Editor of the Saturday newspaper. He said his aim was to have me edit one of the THISDAY titles in due course. I was not properly disposed to the redeployment, but I accepted it because of the grace and candour with which he approached me. Obaigbena was in the habit of redeploying people without consulting them. But he did not treat me that way. I felt privileged that he handled my own case differently.

But not too long afterwards, Obaigbena had cause to move me again. This time as Deputy Editor of the Daily newspaper. I remained on this beat until another idea crept in. THISDAY was to start publishing an ambitious, all-colour, all-gloss magazine called Leaders & Co. I was appointed the Editor of the publication. A team was constituted for the magazine and it took off in earnest.

The first edition came out rich, bright and beautiful. So were subsequent editions. A number of editions were produced and circulated. Then there was a lull. The cost of printing the all-colour and glossy magazine at that time was becoming prohibitive. The newspaper house had a problem coping with the bills from

Academy Press, our printers. As a stop-gap measure, the magazine was converted to a newspaper which would circulate as an insert in the Saturday newspaper. A few more editions were produced and inserted. But after sometime, the newspaper house began to show signs that the publication could not be sustained. That notwithstanding, we produced more and more editions which were never printed. This went on for sometime until the magazine was rested. That was at the end of the year 2000. The magazine, as it were, went with the last millennium.

At the turn of the century in January, 2001, I got my last redeployment at THISDAY. This time as the Editorial Page Editor. I held this position until I left the employ of the newspaper in 2003.

Chapter 9

BIRTH OF BROKEN TONGUES

One of the enduring innovations which Obaigbena introduced into the Nigerian Newspaper industry is the back page column. I wrote my first column in THISDAY in 1997 when I became the Deputy Editorial Page Editor. The column ran for as long as I was on the Editorial Board. But by September 1999 or thereabout, Obaigbena came up with the idea of having columns placed strategically on the back page of the newspaper. The columns were to be made prominent by giving them titles and putting the columnists' photographs on them. It was a marketing strategy which THISDAY wanted to use to have an edge over other Nigerian newspapers. A few senior Editors were selected to pioneer the back page column. I was one of the editors selected. Everybody was at liberty to give his column the title he deemed fit.

As a literary scholar, I went into creative thinking to be able to fashion out a name for my column. The critical reflection took me back in time to 1986. An International literary conference had held then at the University of Lagos. I was an undergraduate in the Department of English of the university at that time. I attended the conference and listened to various speakers that came from across the globe. One of the presenters, a foreigner from either the Caribbean or the black American community in the United States, had harped on a theme on division and separatism which usually afflicted Africans who were uprooted from the African soil and forcibly taken to foreign lands where they became slaves. The status of the African male as an upside down man, more often than not, created cleavages in the home front. There was hardly any unity of purpose. Families began to speak in broken tongues and this, invariably, led to a number of broken homes. Broken tongues, in the sense in which it is used here, could connote disunity, fractiousness, absence of unanimity of purpose or the like. It could also be interpreted to mean a corrupted and diluted version of the English Language or a blackness of the tongue; something that William Labov, an American linguist widely regarded as the founder of the discipline of Variationist sociolinguistics, described as Black English Vernacular.[12] This play on words and juggling of meanings appealed to me in its own way. It was my reflection on and appreciation of this pun that I was later to conceive as "Broken Tongues".

The coinage is a reflection of the fact that broken tongues usually lead to broken homes. BROKEN TONGUES is therefore imagistic. It was borne out of my critical responses to and appreciation of the way Literature functions especially in a multi-cultural setting such as the one the African male and female found themselves in as slaves. It is also an apt reflection on the fractiousness that is the Nigerian environment. The coinage did not therefore come about by mere coupling of words. It is a creative endeavour. It is a coinage whose meaning and significance lurk in the deepest recesses of my creative imagination. That is why I am passionate about it. It is, indeed, my own version of R.B. Sheridan's "Circulating Library"[13]. Something Sheridan calls the evergreen tree of diabolical knowledge. BROKEN TONGUES is like my muse. It has an embedded meaning and connotation which can best be appreciated by creative minds. The connotation can also be protean. There is nothing static about it. What matters is that it goes beyond the ordinary. The knowledge associated with it may not be diabolical in the sense Sheridan talks about his circulating library. But it has an evergreen dimension because at every point in time, it mirrors issues that have immediacy of appeal. BROKEN TONGUES signifies all of this and more. Even though I adopted it as a newspaper column, BROKEN TONGUES is, indeed, more than a column. It is an idea; it is a living, throbbing imagination.

As a column, BROKEN TONGUES has, without doubt, acquired a life of its own. It is a subject of discourse in intellectual and educated circles, and even beyond. The body of works has become a veritable reference material for scholars and researchers. In November 2007, for instance, a Bachelor of Arts Long Essay was submitted to the Department of English and Literature of Abia State University by Miss Comfort Onwuekwe. The title of the Long Essay was "A Study of Style and Effective Writing in Dr. Amanze Obi's Selected Essays". The essays in question were all taken from the corpus of my articles written under the banner of BROKEN TONGUES. My projection is that some day, a novel of ideas entitled BROKEN TONGUES which has been incubating in my imagination will come to light.

Significantly, I have had occasion to give life to the idea long before it became a column. As the Features Editor of Third Eye newspapers in 1995, I combined the position with column-writing. I also sat on the Editorial Board of the newspaper. One of the articles I wrote for the newspaper at that time mirrored my mental romance with the idea of Broken Tongues. The article published in Third Eye Daily of 22nd August, 1995, was entitled "Broken tongues, Broken homes." Below is how I used the underlying significance of the poetic image to present my argument.

"If the ongoing frantic efforts at gender-bending is part of our preparations for the challenges of the 21st Century, then there is every reason to believe that the family unit in Nigeria is still at its rudimentary best. Again, if the hysteria that usually attends

Nigeria's attempts at being identified with global rat races is brought to bear on the quest for the rights of women, then we should expect an atomization of the family consciousness that will be both bemusing and benumbing. This will be especially so given the fact that Nigeria has no remarkable record in women activism.

"When Mary Wollstonecraft blazed the trail sometime in the 18th Century, her encapsulation of the rights of women was based on her experiences in the English society of her time. When Sojourner Truth, the fiery American activist, debunked the claim in male circles that women were incapable of assuming certain responsibilities, she based her argument on the reality of her environment. Even Betty Friedan's systematic deconstruction of the cultural myths and attitudes towards women was based on her perception of the American society of the twentieth century.

"Although Wollstonecraft, Truth and Friedan seemed to capture the experiences of women generically, they were, as a matter of fact, crusading for the environments with which they were familiar. In fact, it is significant to note that their efforts were accentuated by the feminist fervour which took the later part of the twentieth century by storm. There were complaints from feminist circles that the English Language is sexist. They saw it as a male language which made it possible for men to dominate discourse.

"To counter male control of discourse then, the French Feminists took the issue a step further when they took female language to the level of the sublime. For them, contrary to the widely held notion that women's reasoning is, more often than not, child-like, the French feminists settled for the sublime mode of writing which they felt would rescue women and their writings from the charge of weakness.

"However, to discerning African minds, these were European and American responses to matters of gender. When therefore the likes of Alice Walker, an African-American novelist, chose to talk about feminism, she recognised that it was no use starting from where white women stopped. For her, the black woman was left out even in the feminist crusade of suffragettes like Wollstonecraft and Friedan. It was for this reason that she chose not to call herself a feminist but a "womanist" because it is the latter that captures the black woman's peculiar experience.

"Obviously, the United Nations Development Programmme (UNDP) did not take cognizance of continental or racial divergences when it carried out its survey on gender bias in 174 countries of the world in its 1995 report. The report which was released last week stated that the level of participation by women in political and economic affairs was lowest in Africa. The Nordic nations of Sweden, Norway, Finland and Denmark were identified as the most sexually egalitarian in the world.

"The indices which the UNDP employed in its survey are not quite well known to me, but it is doubtful if the survey attempted a sociological reading of the peoples of the countries which the report purportedly covered. If this was done, it would have been clear to UNDP that matters of gender are largely suigeneris and hardly admit of generalisations. In a country like Nigeria where benevolent sexism is the order of the day, it should be expected that the woman who benefits very immensely from the protective role of the man should concede certain rights to him. This would be quite unlike what obtains in most western societies where sex roles are being redefined on the basis of cultural practices that are decidedly anti-woman. Perhaps, the report, released at this time, is meant to prepare grounds for the Beijing summit on women.

In less than two weeks from today, those who see themselves as representatives of Nigerian women will be in Beijing, China, for the fourth United Nations conference on women. As a prelude to that, the Minister of Women Affairs and Social Development, Ambassador Judith Attah, last week in Abuja indicated that a document on how to improve the lot of Nigerian women would be presented at the Beijing conference which will appraise the advancement of women in all spheres of life.

"If experience of the world is anything to go by, it should be clear to our women representatives that a holistic pursuit of policy matters is ultimately counter-productive. There are as many variations as there are entities and nationalities. It will be misleading then to expect that the conference should make a blanket recommendation on the way forward for women. Regional, racial, continental and other variables must be brought into play. A situation where the UNDP is interested in carrying out a gender-specific index of human development is, in itself, a segregationist agenda. If the affairs of the world are so mapped out, the danger is there that an unnecessary suspicion will be created between the sexes. When this is the case, development agenda will be gender-based. This was what Ambassador Attah hinted at when she alluded to a woman's development agenda for the 21st Century.

"The dangers inherent in this outlook look frightening to me. I envisage a situation where the man and woman in the house will be pursuing divergent agenda. Situations such as this have largely led to the phenomenon called broken tongues in American society. And it has consequently led to broken homes.

"As my worry congeals into morbid fear, it is salutary to recognise that there are still the sane ones among Nigerian women who recognise the boundaries that must remain sacrosanct. Such women recognise and acknowledge that women's attempt at redefining society may be working perfectly well in the offices but have failed woefully in the homes. Perhaps, it is when our women are able to draw a line between the home and the office that they will recognise the limits of their empowerment."[14]

The above article gives you a peep into my bias for Gender Studies which my Ph.D thesis faithfully mirrors. But it goes beyond that. It is a living, breathing proof that "Broken Tongues" predates 1999 when it began to appear in THISDAY as a column. That is why I find it regrettable that BROKEN TONGUES, my creative endeavour, was to become a subject of litigation at some point in my career.

As a newspaper column, BROKEN TONGUES first appeared in THISDAY in September 1999. It ran in the newspaper as a weekly column until May 2003. When I left THISDAY, the column moved over to THE SUN newspapers in June 2003. It went on recess in February 2009 upon my appointment as Honourable Commissioner in the government of Imo State. It returned to THE SUN in August 2011 after my tour of duty as commissioner and resumed the column.

Chapter 10

BRIDE OF THE SUN

After nearly seven years of writing for THISDAY, I had come to acquire fame and prominence. BROKEN TONGUES had, in a way, launched me into stardom. I became very much sought after by policy makers in and out of government. I was also the toast of many cerebral newspaper readers. Given this state of affairs, THISDAY had become for me a comfort zone just as BROKEN TONGUES had become a prized possession. I needed to keep it running in order to continue to occupy that enviable position in the ranking of the reading public. When therefore Orji Uzor Kalu, then Governor of Abia State, approached me to join his yet-to-be- published newspaper, THE SUN, I sneered at the proposal. I dismissed it as a huge joke.

Before Kalu's move, many newspaper publishers had approached me to help pioneer their nascent publications. I turned down all the offers because they did not, in my estimation, hold any promise for me. Kalu's was therefore one of the many offers that came my way. But I was not the only one at THISDAY at that time that Kalu wooed. The others who did not have the kind of hang-up I had made up their minds early enough and had to join the pioneer team that started off the newspaper. When Kalu persisted and even made some offers to me as a form of enticement, I was still amused at the whole thing. But at some point, I had to introduce the matter to my wife. We debated it for weeks on end. In fact, leaving THISDAY for THE SUN was one of the most difficult decisions I ever took in my career as a journalist. It tasked me mentally.

I considered the fact of the newness of THE SUN as well as the fact that the acceptance of the newspaper by the reading public was not guaranteed as a huge disincentive. I did not also lose sight of the fact that in journalism, the medium makes the message and that if you write the best of stories and nobody reads them owing to the obscurity of the medium in which they appear, then your effort would have amounted to nothing. I was afraid that I could go into oblivion if I began to write for a newspaper that nobody would read. I imagined a situation where my fame would peter out if I leave the known medium for an unknown one. Why on earth should I willingly choose to go into oblivion with my eyes wide open? The answer to this question, whatever it was, engaged me intermittently.

As I battled with myself, Kalu also plotted his way through. His offer came in many forms. He even offered a Mercedes C – Class as my official car. I had gone to see him at his Victoria Island residence on his invitation only to be presented with the keys to the car. I could not reject the offer. It would have been rude to do so. It would have amounted to disrespect for the governor. I accepted the keys and got someone among his pool of drivers to follow me with the car to THISDAY corporate headquarters in Apapa. When we arrived at THISDAY, I parked my own car and went home with the C- Class that night. But collecting the keys of the car and driving it away did not, for me, mean the acceptance of Kalu's invitation to work for THE SUN. I continued the debate with my wife. While all this was going on, I ensured that I did not use the car. My consideration was that I would return the car to Kalu, if at the end of the day, I rejected the offer.

As part of the process of taking a decision on whether to work with THE SUN or not, I had taken time off, on Kalu's advice, to go and see Mike Awoyinfa and Dimgba Igwe who were the Managing Director and Deputy Managing Director respectively of the newspaper. That was at their temporary base on Osolo way, Isolo. At the meeting, Dimgba had asked me if I was interested in editing one of the titles of the newspaper. I told him I was not. I preferred to remain on the Editorial Board. As a Ph.D holder, I did not think that a newspaper house was a good place to be. But having found myself in one, I needed to distance myself as much as possible from the howl and madness of the Newsroom as that would take me further away from intellectual engagements. Even though I did not think that a newspaper house, generally speaking, was befitting enough for me, I considered the Editorial Board a bit tolerable. That informed my choice.

Dimgba was, at that point, still trying to appoint Editors for the three titles of the newspaper. Steve Nwosu, who had just left THISDAY in controversial circumstances at that time, was being considered for editorship of one of the titles. But Dimgba's mind was not made up either to engage him for that position or not. He asked me to tell him about this Steve whom Nduka Obaigbena had just disowned and written off publicly as incompetent. I told Dimgba that Steve was competent enough and that he should disregard what Obaigbena said of him. I made Dimgba to understand that Obaigbena's statement on Steve was done for purposes of expediency- to assuage the anger of some Moslem faithful who felt that the title Steve edited at THISDAY blasphemed prophet Mohammed.

Shortly after my visit to Osolo Way, Dimgba prepared my letter of appointment. I was to assume duties on 1st of May, 2003. But I told Dimgba that I was not ready yet. I told him that I would be ready on 1st of June. For me, the one month extension would afford me the final opportunity to make up my mind either to accept or reject the offer. But because Nature has a way of resolving internal conflicts in individuals, something akin to a deus ex machina crept into the scene and helped to resolve my many months of indecision. Something that gave me mixed feelings took place at THISDAY at that point in time and it simply helped me to take a decision on the issue at stake. I decided to take the leap in the dark, whatever it was worth. That was how I came to join the staff of THE SUN on June 1st, 2003, as Chairman of the Editorial Board.

Chapter 11

CREATING THE SUN BACK PAGE COLUMN

Two weeks after joining THE SUN, the newspaper went daily. But I was still keeping my column under wraps. I did not want to launch it carelessly on the pages of THE SUN without impact. The newspaper at the time did not have back page columns. It was not part of the consideration of the Management of the newspaper. The pioneers of the newspaper conceived it strictly as a soft sell. They did not want anything serious to grace the pages of the newspaper. Instead, their bent tended towards the hilarious and the sensational. A back page column that dissects issues of national importance would, it was imagined, give the newspaper a serious outlook that would deviate from its tabloid concept. Since I was not, by training, a fan of soft sell journalism, I was not prepared to immerse myself into that tradition. So, I made moves to, at least, find a balance between what the newspaper was conceived to be and my own preferences and idiosyncrasies as a serious-minded writer.

Fully aware that there was no prominent writer among the flock at THE SUN who would be as passionate about the back page column as myself, I did not bother to discuss the issue of columns at Management Committee level. I knew that a good many of them would not be properly disposed to my position on the matter.

Consequently, I went back to Kalu to discuss the matter. I made him understand why we needed to have back page columns. I told him that if part of his objective was to attract known writers like me to give his newspaper credibility and acceptability, then we needed to achieve this fast by strategically positioning the columns that people would like to identify with. Kalu accepted my proposal but asked me if I had discussed it with Dimgba. I told him I had not. He then called Dimgba there and then and began to tell him why back page column should be introduced in the Newspaper. Dimgba, from what I gathered from the conversation, tried to resist the idea. But Kalu impressed the idea further on him. Dimgba eventually gave in. That was how the back page column came to be introduced in The SUN.

With that arrangement in place, I then released BROKEN TONGUES on the back page of THE SUN. Luckily for all of us, the newspaper did not have the problem of acceptability. Apart from the few serious segments which columns such as mine represented, the newspaper was largely a soft sell. It was almost a wholesale transplant of THE SUN of London. The Nigerian reading public had not seen anything like it before. Mike Awoyinfa used his tabloid bent to spice up the newspaper. Sensationalism was its mainstay. This hit the Nigerian newspaper market like a storm.

But if a segment of the readership was going to protest or recoil at this, it was quickly neutralized or balanced with serious features such as the columns and the editorials that I midwifed. Before I joined THE SUN, the editorials of the newspaper were too brief and the style of presentation too pedestrian to be taken seriously by perceptive readers. I changed all of that and brought seriousness and depth to bear on the editorials. In fact, the newspaper, at inception, was an admixture of the mundane and the serious. But with the blend and some form of editorial reengineering, the marriage turned out to be an instant success.

Chapter 12

TRAVELLING FOR THE SUN

Having succeeded in attracting me to THE SUN, Kalu did not turn his attention away from me instantly. He still worked hard enough to consolidate his hold on me. I had joined THE SUN team as his special nominee. He had to demonstrate that he did not bring me to THE SUN for the sake of it. He therefore took his effort a notch further by taking me on foreign trips. The overall objective was to offer me something different from what obtained at my last place of work.

It all began with a trip with him and Mike Awoyinfa across the West Coast of Africa. A chartered aircraft had air-lifted us from the presidential wing of the Murtala Muhammed Airport Lagos to Freetown, Sierra Leone. Kalu was on a business trip to oversee his banks and insurance companies across the West Coast. When that was over, we went on a courtesy call to the Presidential Villa where we met with and interviewed President Tejan Kabbah, the then President of the country. Days later, we moved over to Banjul, The Gambia, to the warm welcome of Serekunda, the beautiful resort that makes the country one of the most visited in West Africa. A major highlight of our stay in Banjul was the visit to the State House where we met with and also interviewed President Yahyah Jammeh. At the end of the trip, I summed up my impressions in an article published in THE SUN of June 26, 2003, entitled: "From

Freetown to Banjul with mixed feelings". Aspects of the article read thus:

"The story of Africa, strictly speaking, has not left the stage of lamentation. Here in Nigeria, we are given to comparing notes. We do not hesitate in reminding ourselves that things work a lot better in Europe and America. Each time we lament over our backwardness, we do it with a tinge of sanctimoniousness. We try to impress it upon ourselves that the problem does not lie in us, but in something outside of us. We like to pass the buck, and that partly explains why we keep hoping, without actually making an impact in the right direction, that things would change for the better. Therein lies our seemingly perpetual habitation in a self-imposed state of potency.

"But if Nigeria suffers from home-grown, if not congenital disabilities, their brothers in some other parts of Africa have a different kind of headache to grapple with. My recent association with Sierra Leoneans and Gambians in their respective capital cities – Freetown and Banjul – tells the story of a people who are still searching desperately for an identity they can be proud of.

"Freetown, the land of slaves, is still bogged down by a slavish mentality. From the outlook of the city to the nature of business activities, you would be confronted with a people struggling to give their life some meaning. Freetown is still being haunted by the foreign influence that bred slavery in the past. After years of fratricidal strife in Sierra Leone, the people have come to distrust themselves to the point that they readily and willingly latch onto foreign assistance and manipulation. The quick succession with which characters like Joseph Momoh, Valentine Strasser, Foday Sankoh, Julius Maada Bio, Jonny Koromah and Tejan Kabbah have played the game of musical chairs in the country simply tells the story of a fractious people in dire search for an integer.

"Before now, the people found some succour in the ECOWAS Monitoring Group known as ECOMOG. It was ECOMOG that defeated the forces loyal to Komorah after he forcefully seized power from Kabbah on May 25, 1997. But the restoration of the government of Tejan Kabbah on March 10, 1998 only brought a tenuous peace. Today, the country is still standing on a precipice. The people are therefore still being protected by a foreign influence.

"In the absence of ECOMOG, the United Nations (UN) has taken over. The presence of UN forces, vehicles, aircraft and other equipment in Freetown is simply frightening. Beginning from the Lungi Airport in Freetown, the impression you get is that the country is run by an army of occupation. Following the skirmishes in the country, many who would have loved to do business there are retreating. This state of affairs has, naturally, affected the volume of air traffic to Freetown. With Lungi airport largely stripped of commercial aircraft from other countries, UN fighter planes are what you see.

"Then, when you finally enter the city of Freetown proper with the aid of rickety helicopters which look as if they would drop into the sea, you will be welcomed by UN jeeps and other combat vehicles. They parade the undulating landscape of the city, leaving you wondering whether Sierra Leone is a UN-administered territory. The siege is, indeed, total.

"The newly commissioned high class hotel in the city, Bintumani Hotel, is equally peopled by these UN forces. Their camouflage uniforms would readily remind a Nigerian of the days of Biafra. Yet, we are talking about Sierra Leone of the 20th Century. A set-up such as this casts a slur on the efforts being made by the government in Sierra Leone to bring about a positive difference in the land.

"Agriculture, for instance, is the centre of the economy of the country. So is diamond. With a huge array of fertile arable land and plenty of water to go with it, Sierra Leone aspires to go beyond subsistence in food production. To ensure the realization of this objective, the government of Tejan Kabbah has entered into an agreement with the United States, the European Union and the Commonwealth on the possibility of exporting food from Sierra Leone. However, the sad impediment remains the sporadic shootings that have left what is supposed to be Freetown's city centre groveling on its belly. With the lull in business activities, the vitality of the people is equally subdued.

"The situation in Banjul is not one of war. But it still revolves around underdevelopment, largely occasioned by foreign influence. To begin with, the country does not carry a huge burden. It has a population of less than one million. Its land mass is equally not vast. What President Yahyah Jammeh has tried to do is to open up the hinterland. He is doing this through an aggressive road development programme.

"Jammeh believes he has an answer to the country's problems. To demonstrate this conviction, a big board bearing Jammeh's portrait with the inscription "With You All the Way," is what welcomes you to the State House. The confidence reposed in the president has equally been demonstrated with the establishment of the Jammeh Foundation for Peace.

"However, for Gambians, these amount to mere tokenism. A significant population of Gambians still see their president as a man with tyrannical disposition. They are not happy that the better part of aids from donor agencies are no longer being directed to food. For a people who are not given to hard work, the new policy of development of infrastructure by the government of the day is a policy of starvation of the people. They are therefore sad. In response to their complaints, government has set up a scheme called National Youth Services Scheme where youths are encouraged to acquire skills in plumbing, art and craft, mechanics and electricity, among others. The development of infrastructure has also seen the government expanding its tourism base and maximizing the potentials. The Kairaba Beach Hotel epitomizes the suitability of The Gambia in the area of tourism. But the caveat still remains. Tourism in the land is dominated and influenced by white folks. The average Gambian still remains a second class citizen even in his country. The only university in the country is run by foreigners, including Nigerians. But the people do not look bothered. Thus, from Freetown to Banjul, you are trailed by the slavish mentality of a people who look too willing to be recolonized."[15]

That was how I summarized my impressions about the two West African countries. Those were exciting times. The trips provided me with a story bank. With them, I kept my columns smoking hot with juicy reportage. I actually maintained two columns in The Sun at that time. Apart from BROKEN TONGUES which was published every Monday then, I ran another column on Thursdays in the inside page of the newspaper.

Chapter 13

AT HOME WITH MANDELA

Two months after the trip to the West Coast, that is by August, 2003, we were on another trip. This time to South Africa. Mike Awoyinfa was also on the trip. We traversed Johannesburg and Pretoria. We were at State House Pretoria to see the then President, Thabo Mbeki. We also had interview with him. Before then, Mike and I had been taken to the headquarters of the African National Congress (ANC) where we had sessions with prominent party officials culminating in an interview with Kgalema Petrus Motlanthe who, years later, was to become the transition president of South Africa from 25th September, 2008 to 9th May, 2009.

But the highpoint of our visit to South Africa remained our meeting with the legendary Nelson Mandela. I was late to the meeting. The night before we were to have the interview with Mandela, Mike and I, in the company of three or four others on Kalu's entourage, were at two different Night Clubs in Johannesburg. After all the carousing, we returned to our hotel rooms in the early hours of the morning. We went into deep sleep moments later. But at about 8 am, the intercom in my room rang. "His Excellency is downstairs", I was told. That meant that we should join Kalu immediately for the meeting with Mandela. Mike whose room was next to mine dressed up immediately without bathing and ran downstairs to meet with the team. I insisted on bathing before dressing up. By the time I was downstairs, I only met a car and a driver waiting for me. Mike managed to catch up with the rest of the team.

The team which included Orji Kalu himself was ushered in to see Mandela as soon as they got to the legend's house. I was yet to arrive. A clear instruction was therefore left at the gate that I should be let in as soon as I arrived. That was done. I met the team half way into the interview . I felt somewhat awkward that I was not there at the beginning. When I tried to apologize for my lateness, Kalu retorted thus: "Whatever happens to a man is for his own good". That was his usual refrain. Regardless of that, the memory of our visit to Mandela was, for me, one for all times. It humanised the iconic sage whom the entire globe adored for good reasons.

Again, I summarized my impressions about South Africa in the article published in THE SUN of August 18, 2003, entitled: "This is State House Pretoria." It reads:

"This State House, otherwise known as Mahlamba Ndlopfu, has quartered many presidents of the Republic of South Africa. Its immediate past occupant was the legend called Nelson Rolihlahla Mandela. And now it is inhabited by the father figure known as Thabo Mbeki.

"To tell the story of this house is to capture the essential leadership that South Africa has been blessed with since the first all-race elections took place in the country in 1994. The first thing that compels attention about this house is its gothic trappings. The architecture is like a development of the earliest Romanesque which flourished in Europe between 12th and 15th centuries. Its ogival arch, elaborate stone vaulted roofs and rich stone carvings, among others, give an impression of medieval spirituality. The building is devoid of flamboyance. Its simplicity stands in contradistinction with the power and influence government symbolizes.

"No doubt, government is about power and influence. This is especially so in third world countries. But the tendency is particularly manifest in Africa, yet the structure which shelters the presidents of Africa's most respected and admired country is devoid of such fetish. Invariably, its occupant has come to be at one with its unpretentiousness. Only two gates sparsely manned by courteous guards take you to this house without being harassed or your sight assaulted by gun-totting, insolent and overzealous guards.

"To a large extent, the house looks unpeopled. The hustle and the bustle which government houses in Nigeria are associated with are completely absent here. There are no hangers-on. No office or contract seekers. No gossips. Ubiquitous party men are not there. In fact, the quietness of the place borders on desolation. Indeed, the house may look isolated. It may look idle, even deserted. But it is, in reality, one of the engine rooms that responsible and responsive governance can boast of. From this quiet coven, the Republic of South Africa, since the emergence of black rule almost a decade ago, has held itself together.

"Having inherited a tradition of order and decency in governmental and corporate affairs, the black majority which wrested power from white minority after some 350 years of white supremacist rule, can be said to have lived up to expectation. They have not disappointed those outside South Africa who felt, argued, and fought for the emancipation of the black community from the clutches of apartheid.

"My recent trip to South Africa in the company of Mike Awoyinfa, my colleague at THE SUN, where we held separate audiences with Mandela and Mbeki reveals a lot about the depth of intellect and humanity of these icons of leadership. The Mbeki we encountered at Mahlamba Ndlopfu, Pretoria, looked as if he was at peace with his environment. But if we merely suspected so, we got convinced that he was a master of his environment when we began to read his lips and his mind over dinner. It is the close of winter in South Africa and freezing cold had driven many into cold corners that Friday evening. President Mbeki had his rich textured cardigan in obedience to the demands of the elements. But the cold winter did not distract him from being his essential self.

"His approach to issues African were measured and well thought-out. Each time he was confronted with the oddities in Nigeria, he would not chuckle. Even when he showed surprise, he did so without betraying any serious emotion. You could neither accuse him of mischief nor disinterest. He also did not relapse into ignoble ease. As a good listener, Mbeki would take in all your points, run his racing thought through them, and then begin to interject in a manner that can only fit the sagging spirit of a long-distance runner.

"He did so when we were attempting a post mortem on the 2003 general elections in Nigeria. The pre-eminent role he played in President Olusegun Obasanjo's quest for second term, the post-election petitions of General Muhamadu Buhari (rtd.), and related issues, all came up for mention. Anybody who is conversant with the political and diplomatic undercurrents that saw Obasanjo back in power in 2003 would appreciate the fact that Mbeki was a central figure in this matter. Yet when he joins issues with you, you will almost pass him off as a disinterested, if not unconcerned observer. Each time he wanted to interject, he would first smile wryly and then make his point without betraying any emotions. He is not given to throwing his listeners into emotional lows and highs.

"If there is any emotion at all in his speech, it is controlled to the extent that nothing is betrayed. Sometimes, in the course of our chat, I tried to read stoicism in him, but the impression could not stick. The man is, by no means, a stoic. He is only a tame and cultured fellow whose approach to issues recognizes and appreciates the various tendencies that make up the human community. With that recognition and appreciation, he goes on to make allowances for the various traits and tendencies that make up the human spirit. In the final analysis, what you see is a personality that lets beings be, an eclectic spirit that diffuses the hot and the cold, the wild and the tame. This blend is what president Mbeki considers the ideal. It is a point of view he radiates without preaching it. He counsels it without being obtrusive in his approach.

"So, why is Mbeki such a gentle and genteel spirit? Why does he appear not to be in a hurry in any issue? A little bit of South Africa's experience will suffice. As member of the African National Congress (ANC), the party that fought apartheid to its grave, Mbeki must have learnt so much from some of the freedom fighters within the party who made things happen. As a son of a former leader of ANC, the younger Mbeki must have grown to appreciate that freedom, indeed great human ideals, are achieved not by force of arms, but through intellectual rationalization and dialogue. Over the years, the ANC withstood the storm from the white overlords without engaging them in deadly or brutal assault. The Albert Luthulis, the Oliver Thambos, the J.l. Dubes and others and the Nelson Mandelas of ANC, among others, did not take up arms against the system that oppressed them. Their staying power was affirmative action. They preferred dialogue to disruption. Whereas the system devised new ways and means to put them down, they countered them by rigorously engaging their intellect. Through such rigour, they were able to come up with a counterpoise. In the end, freedom was achieved without the destruction of infrastructure or loss of lives. The aesthetic beauty of South Africa as we know it today is a product of this resilient spirit. The white overlords developed both the cities and the suburbs at the expense of the black majority. Whites did so because their investments in this regard guaranteed profit. The vices they perpetrated were necessary conditions for the investments to flourish. After centuries of white domination, the generations of black South Africans that fought against the system now have something to look up to. The massive infrastructures put up by the whites are there today. The people relish them. So do visitors from other lands. Thus, what was created by the minority at the expense of the majority was preserved. It stands today as the legacy of hope on which future South Africa must stand.

"President Mbeki did not have to take us through this lecture of profit and loss. He did not have to breathe so hard on anybody to appreciate where his people are coming from and why we should think hard on our own condition in Nigeria. What he does instead is to take you through a route that will leave you wondering whether you are actually sharing these moments with the president of a country that occupies a pride of place in the comity of nations. Upon the realisation that you have been regaled with simplicity and graceful candour both by the house and its occupants, you are then left to yourself to ponder what has gone wrong with your own arrangement back home. In a way then, the dinner we had with Mbeki was more than the sauce that wetted our appetites. It was food for thought. It was a subtle way of impressing it on us that we cannot seek too far to find the tree for the woods. The whole interaction tended to say that we should not be shouting from the roof tops. We should rather bow our heads in deep-seated contemplation. That way, we shall, like William Golding's marooned children in Lord of the Flies, discover why things are what they are. Perhaps when we do, we shall weep for the death of the ideals of the founding fathers of this land. Perhaps then too, we shall rediscover ourselves for a better tomorrow. Mahlamba

Ndlopfu, Pretoria, the house from where president Mbeki's rich intellect flows, teaches all this. And more."[16]

This was the South Africa that I encountered in 2003. When Mandela died 10 years later, I was filled me with nostalgia. There was so much to remember; so much to talk about.

Chapter 14

GOING TO AMERICA

The year 2005 presented yet another opportunity for a foreign trip with Kalu, this time to the United States of America. The 2007 elections were approaching. Kalu was on the second lap of his governorship then. He had started looking beyond Abia State and had indicated interest in running for the presidency. Our trip to the United States was to sensitize the international community on his presidential ambition. From Washington D.C. to Chicago, Nigeria's presidential campaign message as enunciated by Kalu resonated.

But beyond the Kalu campaigns, I was privileged to have a global view of the society that we encountered. My impressions, captured in an article entitled "America and the Lincoln Mystique" published in the WEEKLY SPECTATOR of November 13, 2005, reads thus:

"A seven and a half-hour long flight from London had taken us to Dulles International Airport, Washington, D.C., United States of America. We had touched down right on time for a public lecture at the Woodrow Wilson Centre in Washington. But to be a part of the lecture, we had to engage in a duel with time. A trick of fate had made all the difference. Immigration and security checks at Dulles played the spoilsport. I had an easy passage at the immigration point. But not so with my colleague.

United States intelligence agents at the airport needed to carry out further scrutiny of him and his mission. Coming at a time London was held hostage by terrorists, any flight originating from London was closely watched, and the passengers were carefully screened. This was the lot of my companion. Consequently, he was "quarantined" in an inner chamber while his documents and records went through intelligence scrutiny. I waited with him with baited breath. When he was eventually released from "detention", a sniffer dog was unleashed on us. By the time we left the airport, we had lost valuable man hours that ate deeply into our time.

"Regardless of the distraction at Dulles, Washington embraced us with its warmth and serenity. The journey from Dulles to River Road, Potomac, an upper class settlement in Maryland, laid American orderliness bare. Despite the long traffic that we faced, everybody retained his sanity, thus divesting the journey of tension and tedium. You could almost associate the mood in the city with the passivity that was the essential nature of Abraham Lincoln , one of the youngest American presidents in history who worked so hard to preserve the Union. As you journey on into the heart of Washington, you are confronted more with the tales and signs of Lincoln, a mythic figure whose image graces stamps and statues.

"America remembers Lincoln as one of its greats. He was a quintessential American dreamer who rose from the patches of poverty to the power and influence of the American Presidency. This power and influence would readily beckon you as you confront the symbols of American commanding heights in world affairs. The White House, the Capitol Hill, the Union Station, the House of Representatives and Senate Building and the Lincoln Memorial define American influence and place in history.

Even though America stands tall today as symbolized by these imposing monuments as well as by the influence it wields in the international arena, the country was not made great. Rather, it achieved greatness. The heights reached and kept by Lincoln followed this trajectory. Lincoln had a very humble background. He had no past to be proud of. He therefore led his life regardless of what his ancestry was. He worked hard to make himself what he is remembered for today in history. While he lived, and while he presided over affairs at the White House, Lincoln refused to be bogged down by received notions and beliefs. He confronted situations as they came. As a Calvinist, he believed in predestination and worked tirelessly in the evolution of a better world. This tendency led him to emancipate the slaves in America. As America grows in power and influence, the Lincoln mystique hovers around its horizon, helping to point the way. A life of freedom which America is known for derives largely from the Lincoln influence.

Thus, after the airport experience, we decided to feel free, but not dangerously so. This feeling found expression in our gyrations at Tradewinds Nite Club in Maryland. It was a free-wheeling, easy-going environment where the old, the middle-aged and the young had a field day. They mixed freely one with another dancing away in delirium. Even though this was the case, I was not fascinated by what I saw. There was a complete absence of seductive and succulent ladies trying their hands on bacchanal exposure. However, I was to be told later by those who know the city better that the club we patronized was not one to celebrate the foibles and exaggerations of youth".

Chapter 15

LAND OF LINCOLN

"This is Chicago, in the State of Illinois. It is fondly referred to as "Land of Lincoln". After the feverish attempt at capturing the essence of Washington in a matter of days, the call of duty had taken us to Chicago. To do this, we had to return to Dulles International. We were transiting from one part of the United States to another. Surprisingly, however, we went through a security check that made that of our entry from London look like child's play. This time, we were made to off-load most of the things we had on us- jackets, shoes, wrist watches, belts and mobile phones, among others, were removed and tendered on a rolling tray. You are then touched in vital regions all in the bid to know if you are in possession of dangerous objects.

Even though Lagos and London had ignored me and my manicure kit, O'Hare International Airport, Chicago, did otherwise. The security check there had unearthed my kit, discovered my little knife and removed it from the kit. I would not be allowed to board the plane with it. What to do? Who takes it? I was asked to give it to someone at "the other end". There was no such person. O'Hare took possession of it. It was, for me, a bad loss. I had used that kit for eleven years and had continued to savour and cherish its entire content. Now, it has been decapitated, mangled and disfigured, all in the name of American security. It was, perhaps, one price I had to pay for going to the land of Lincoln. It was like embarking on a trip to the land of great discovery.

And if we were curious or expectant, American Airlines, operated by American Eagle, was quite on hand to take us to our destination. Having landed at O'Hare airport, the journey into the heart of Chicago had begun in earnest. But just before the airplane touched down, you could see the ambition in the layout of the city. This land of Lincoln can boast of an array of skyscrapers lined up in a manner that makes the city's skyline look harmonious and radiant. Having produced an Abraham Lincoln who was not interested in his ancestry, Chicago has chosen to claim what belongs to it. If Lincoln was self- effacing, Chicago is too willing to embrace what it has chosen and even declare it openly. This was what Chicago did when it proudly declares itself as the "Land of Lincoln".

But while Lincoln believed that his early life was uneventful and could be summarized in the phrase, " The short and simple annals of the poor", Chicago, the city which has chosen to play back the romantic memories of Lincoln, cannot be so summarized. The city is neither short nor small. It is also not a simple one. The story of Chicago is not the story of the poor. If anything, it is the story of ambition and alertness. Lincoln had traits of ambition, mental alertness and power of analysis in abundance. These were part of the qualities that stood him out. Having left an uncommon legacy of hope and accomplishment behind, Chicago, where his roots lay, could not but identity with him.

In this city of ambition, we were enveloped in the cosy comfort of Hyatt Regency Hotel, O'Hare from where you see and feel the effulgence and munificence of Chicago. From the chauffeur-driven experience we were used to, curiosity had, one day, driven us to try the other life. This was life in the rail tube. We had chosen to explore a train ride in our journey to downtown Chicago. The journey lasted for about one and a half hours, taking us through Indiana, Iowa, Memphis and some other notable spots. But midway into the journey, I suddenly realized that a train could be a target for terrorists as was the case in London sometime in June or thereabout. Upon this realization, I began to scrutinize faces, especially those who joined us at subsequent stopovers. I actually came close to believing that a guy I saw in one of the coaches could be a dangerous character. But my fear was short-lived. He disembarked not too long after I took unusual notice of him.

After a tedious trip to as far as Sheridan Road, and to a mall called T.J Maxx, we decided against train ride on our way back to Hyatt Regency. The return journey was slow but smooth. Almost every intersection was adorned with street lights. And since the rules must be obeyed in God's Own Country, we crawled as much as the traffic allowed. Again, the setting brought back memories and images of passivity which we saw in Washington. It was a trait that Lincoln was known for. But what the American society exhibits is not passivity. It is discipline and the patience to wait for your turn. Everybody in America may be in a hurry, but hardly anyone will be in a hurry to break the rules."17

I was to return to the United States a year later for the World Igbo Congress Convention which held in Boston, Massachusetts. Through that forum, we took Kalu's presidential campaign message to the Igbo in the United States. This trip marked the end of the bridal phase of my sojourn at THE SUN. Within those first three years, I was like the morning rose whose nectar was very much sought after. But after what looked like a honey moon, the party was over. Those who wanted the nectar of the morning rose have had their fill. They began to look the other way. But the rose, in spite of the seeming abandonment, continued to blossom.

Chapter 16

IN RETROSPECT

Looking back, I cannot but underscore issues that are worthy of note in my journalism career. As I noted earlier, my movement at THISDAY was rapid and upward. While with the newspaper, I traversed all branches of journalism. Mr Obaigbena, through the movements and promotions, challenged me to no end to prove my mettle. And at no time did I disappoint.

Besides, Obaigbena's management style, though somewhat unconventional, brought out the best in some of us. You were taught to be independent, to rely less on the day-to-day administration. The environment fired your imagination and taught you self-reliance and creativity. Necessity as the mother of invention was very much at play at THISDAY. The environment was one that tested your creative potentials and challenged you to aspire towards excellence. This was especially so in the light of the fact that Obaigbena gave us a free hand to operate. As mature men and women, we were, of course, not expected to relapse into irresponsibility.

But if there was anything which marked out THISDAY of my time, it was the fact that Mr. Obaigbena never used any columnist or writer to fight his wars. His enemies were not our enemies. He had his circle of friends. And we had ours. His everyday mantra for the newspaper was "No friend, No foe". With this philosophy, we operated freely without fear of being shot down. We also did not have to inherit enemies that we did not create. Thus, after my nearly seven years sojourn at THISDAY, I left without regrets. I did not have to feel that someone has strewn my path with spikes and thorns.

In contrast, my stay at THE SUN, after the initial razzmatazz, was marked by stagnation. It was as if I was baited to the point of immobility. It was then that I realized the beauty of what Obaigbena was doing. Movements, especially upward ones, are capable of bringing out the best in you. But stagnation and closed door approaches could stifle vision and vitiate the process of creativity and innovation. It is not only bad for the personnel, it also leaves the establishment groping with myopia and visionlessness.

However, like Obaigbena, Kalu, as far as I knew him then, did not breathe down on his editors and columnists. He gave them a free hand to operate. But since he is a politician with vested interests that must be protected, those who find themselves working for his newspaper must, without being told, identify those interests and respect them.

Part Three

Government and Politics

Chapter 17

DAWN OF DEMOCRACY

The return of civil rule in 1999 marked a significant turning point in the practice of journalism in Nigeria. Before then, journalism was practised under the repressive atmosphere of military rule. The General Ibrahim Babangida era, for instance, saw to the assassination of Dele Giwa of NEWSWATCH Magazine in 1986. But at no time in the history of the country did the Press face more persecution than the General Sani Abacha regime. It was a period in our national history when newspapers were recklessly proscribed and their premises shut for daring to tell truth to power. Concord Newspapers, The Guardian, and The PUNCH newspapers, among others, were some of the publications that the Abacha regime clamped down on.

However, with the restoration of democratic rule on May 29, 1999, journalism was rescued from the stifling atmosphere of military repression and suppression. Power had changed hands. It had also moved away from repression to liberation. The many years of ceaseless campaign for democracy had ushered in a new democratic spirit. It, to a large extent, threw up a crop of leaders who respected power rather than abuse it. It brought to the fore people who had connected with the people and who appreciate the fact that leadership exists in the service of the people.

As a fairly senior member of the journalism profession at that time, I had the privilege of interfacing and relating with governmental power. And I did that in line with the demands and dictates of my job. On my appointment, for instance, as the Editor of Leaders & Co. under THISDAY stable, I had stepped out in search of people we could truly call leaders. My quest had led me into finding out what some of the governors who had just been elected at that time were doing across the states. In the process, I met and interacted with some of the governors, namely, Abulkadir Kure of Niger state, Peter Odili of Rivers state, Chimaroke Nnamani of Enugu state, Achike Udenwa of Imo state and Orji Uzor Kalu of Abia state, in one fell swoop. I met with some others in my subsequent trips.

The initial contacts may not have made all the impressions on me principally because most of the governors of the time were novices in matters of governance. Some were yet to have a sense of direction at that point in time. Many were, indeed, still under the shadow of military rule. But as the years went by, they began to loosen up in appreciation of the fact that a new dawn had begun. Those who probably were not sure at the beginning that civil rule had come to stay began to fashion out an agenda for governance. Subsequent encounters with these governors and other public office holders began to be more meaningful and engaging. Soon, we were to discover that there were some humble and humane administrators who put the people first before any other thing. I will devote some space here to recount my encounters with just two of them.

The first is Dr Sam Egwu, the Governor of Ebonyi State between 1999 and 2007. By the year 2000, John Otu, my friend and colleague at the University of Lagos, had just bagged his doctorate degree. He joined The Guardian shortly thereafter as a member of the Editorial Board. John was yet to settle down at The Guardian when Governor Egwu discovered the great talent in him and quickly decided to tap into it. The transmutation took place almost like a flash. I had met with John some two weeks earlier. There was no indication that he was about to join the Government of Ebonyi State. Then, the news came. John had become the Commissioner for Information and State Orientation in Ebonyi State. How did it happen? John said he was pleasantly surprised; that he hardly knew the governor. They had met in the recent past at a public forum. Some acquaintanceship took place. Weeks later, John got an invitation to see the Governor. That was how it all happened.

When John told me this, the impression I got was that this governor who would come across a talent, recognize him and equally seek to exploit his intellectual resources must be a people-oriented leader. Based on this impression, I began to like and respect the governor even before I met him. When I eventually met him sometime in 2001, my impressions about him were reinforced. I met a governor who had no airs. He was down-to-earth and clear-headed. I was at home with his personality. Thus, from that time till the time he left office in 2007, I worked as if I was a part of his government. I was, indeed, a part of it in a different sense. Whereas some worked from within, I helped out from outside.

Owing to my positive impression of him, it was little wonder that I, in an article entitled: "Ebonyi: Still Uncorrupted" published in THISDAY of September 5, 2000, had this to say of Governor Egwu. Excerpts....

"Ebonyi, the youngest state in the South East zone of the country, is new in a number of senses. The state is barely three years old. By reasons of geography, it is not quite strategically located. You have to traverse an uneasy terrain to get there. Thus, the state still retains a lot of its virginity. The state is endowed with a number of solid minerals most of which remain untapped. In other words, its flora and fauna have not yet been violated.

"Ebonyi prides itself as the salt of the nation. This is partly because it can boast of a large reservoir of unadulterated, high quality salt. I also believe that Ebonyi so calls itself because of the relative peace which defines life and living in the state. In a country where armed banditry and communal unrest have become a daily fare, a state which witnesses little or none of these can justifiably claim to be the salt which can make others not so specially blessed look green with envy.

"Unlike in most parts of the country where there is a life and death struggle for the spoils of public office, Ebonyi is not yet under the threat of hard-nosed political rascals. Politics in the state still retains an appreciable level of sanity.

"But there is a more interesting aspect to all this. It does appear as if Nature, in its resolve to have Ebonyi retain its saltiness, has decided to thrust upon it a leader who epitomizes all the sanity and decency that go with civilized conduct. The government of Dr Sam Egwu has, since inception, demonstrated in a number of ways that it has a large heart. It is one government which recognizes the essence of public trust and does all it can to uphold it. A case in point is the Nwankwo Kanu Heart Foundation. More than any other state around it, Ebonyi donated very handsomely to the Foundation's trust fund, thus giving a boost to the footballer's laudable initiative. Kanu does not hail from Ebonyi. There is therefore reason to believe that the government in Abakaliki acted on altruistic grounds. Kanu has, interestingly, reciprocated this gesture by choosing Ebonyi as the beneficiary of the Foundation's centre for the South-east zone.

"Another is the appointment of Dr John Otu as the state's Commissioner for Information. John, young and affable and a holder of the Ph.D degree in English from the University of Lagos, qualifies very suitably for the position he now occupies. But that is beside the point. The beauty of his appointment lies in the way it came. John did not have to lobby. He does not even have the power for lobbying. He did not have to enjoy the intervention or recommendation of a traditional ruler. There were no business moguls or moneybags who control their states by proxy that put him forward to hold the office in trust for them. He did not have to be a member of the ruling party in the state. He was not harangued for not being around during the governor's electioneering campaigns.

"What mattered to the governor was the quality of the young man. I would like to believe that Uncle Sam saw in the young John a certain panache and astuteness which a public office holder should possess. The governor, in the manner of a smart bee, went for the nectar.

"To complement the governor's wise choice, the Ebonyi State House of Assembly did not deliberately move to stall the appointment by demanding for gratification as is usually the case in most states of the country. The House encouraged the pollination and the result is the vibrancy that the Ministry now enjoys.

"Unlike most young states which get hooked to their underdog status, Ebonyi has freed itself from debilitating clutches. The state is proactive and outspoken in matters that concern not just the state, but the entire country. When a few months ago the Sharia fire threatened to consume the National Youth Service Corps (NYSC) scheme, Ebonyi was one of the States that rose to the occasion. In the face of the Federal Government's complacency, Ebonyi moved to save its indigenes by offering to institute another service scheme for them in the state. It could be that pre-emptive strikes such as the one from Ebonyi may have clipped the flapping wings of the religious bigots from the Sharia states.

"Ebonyi is ambitious. It is in a hurry to develop. There is, on the part of the government of Egwu, a conscious effort to open the state to the global village. This was demonstrated by the government in May 2000, when it organized an economic summit in Lagos.

The occasion afforded the state the opportunity to showcase its vast solid minerals. The summit also offered prospective investors some understanding of the investment climate in the state.

"But one of the memorable statements at the summit came from the governor. He informed those of us who, owing to lack of familiarity with the state, may think that Ebonyi is as crime-prone as any other state in Nigeria, that the crime rate in the state was below the national average. This drew a lot of laughter from the audience. But the laughter it elicited was not one of derision. It was one of admiration. The statement said a lot about the raw potentials of the state.

"In spite of my admiration for the goings-on in the state, Ebonyi, I believe, will be better appreciated by those who have the opportunity of doing business within its shores. Perhaps it is on the basis of this fact that the Nigeria Union of Journalists (NUJ) in the state, after taking a dispassionate look at Dr. Sam Egwu and the state he presides over, declared him the best governor in the south east zone of the country.

"This award from the NUJ is good for the governor. It is good for the state which produced him. It is also good for the same state, which, even if by default, produced the new President of the Senate, Anyim Pius Anyim. What all these mean is that Ebonyi is opening up. Ebonyi is embracing the larger world. Interestingly, it is doing so without being afflicted by the threadbare and anaemic tradition which define our blighted environment."[18]

This was how I captured my impressions of Ebonyi State under the leadership of Sam Egwu.

The second is Alhaji Attahiru Dalhatu Bafarawa, the good-spirited Governor of Sokoto State from 1999-2007. I first met Bafarawa in 2002 at the Kaduna Trade Fair Complex. He had gone there to deliver a lecture on Northern political agenda under the Olusegun Obasanjo Presidency. I was a witness to the presentation.

I took note of the fine points of his lecture and was later to reflect on them in my column. This was in an article published in THISDAY of April 2, 2002, entitled: "The making of an Arewa point man." It partly reads:

"When Alhaji Attahiru Dalhatu Bafarawa, the Governor of Sokoto State, spoke on the occasion of the second anniversary of the Arewa Consultative Forum last week, he did not speak for himself. He did say that he had the mandate of other Northern governors to speak on their behalf.

"But what did Bafarawa say? The man rolled out a 22-page paper entitled: "Northern Political Agenda: The Way Forward." In it, he carried out a bird's eye view of the pattern of politicking in Nigeria beginning from the First Republic. But because his interest was essentially northern, he touched off the West and East variants of Nigerian politics rather summarily and dwelt instead on the Northern experience.

"Bafarawa told us how the North played the politics of the First Republic. He recalled with nostalgia the noble legacies of the Sardauna of Sokoto and former Premier of Northern Nigeria, Sir Ahmadu Bello. He held aloft the torch of political impregnability which the Sardauna beamed across the north and for which the region was known. But Bafarawa regretted that such northern political cohesion had gone with the winds.

"How did the North come to this crossroads? In the view of Bafarawa, the flight to northern political annihilation was sudden. The First and Second Republics did not, in any way, indicate that the largely monolithic north was about to flounder. During the Second Republic, the National Party of Nigeria (NPN) held the North together just as the Northern Peoples Congress (NPC) did in the First Republic. During the botched Third Republic however, personalities rather than parties mattered, a situation which made it possible for northerners to vote massively for Chief MKO

Abiola of the Social Democratic Party (SDP) while rejecting their kinsman, Alhaji Uthman Tofa. In all this, the north had nothing to regret.

"But all that was then. The coming of Olusegun Obasanjo as civilian president under the present political dispensation has altered the age-old political leaning in the north. As the northern governors who spoke through Bafarawa would have us believe, Obasanjo has dismembered the united north. The north has moved from being one to being fragments. What you have in the north now are mere fractions in dire search for their integers.

"One of the manifestations of this state of affairs is epitomized in the fact that the north, rather than forge a common front under one political party, is balkanized under the Peoples Democratic Party (PDP) and the All Peoples Party (APP). This set-up, the governors said, contrasts sharply with what obtains in the west where the Alliance for Democracy (AD) holds sway and the east where the PDP is completely in charge.

"Bafarawa blames Obasanjo for all this. He recalls the anti-north policies of the Obasanjo administration. He regrets the fact that the president is biting the finger that fed him. In Obasanjo then, the north feels it has made a mistake.

"What then is the way out? According to Bafarawa, the north should, henceforth, realign itself politically with a view to belonging to one party. This is the starting point. Having done that, the north could then work as one united entity with the aim of producing a consensus candidate for the 2003 presidential elections. The candidate being envisaged must be one that would protect the interest of the north. Another way of putting it is to say that the north is prepared to test its political strength again. It appears set to reclaim power. In fact, it wants one of its own to be the president of Nigeria next year.

"So, who is this man to come? And how does the north actualize this pet project? It is instructive to note that the northern point man at the Arewa forum did not emerge from the blues. He was carefully chosen by his people to speak for the entire north in a gathering that paraded eminent northerners like General Yakubu Gowon, General Ibrahim Babangida, Alhaji M.D Yusuf, Alhaji Maitama Sule, Dr Olusola Saraki, Alhaji Abubakar Rimi and Chief Sunday Awoniyi, among others. So far, we have not been told that any northerner of note has raised an eyebrow over Bafarawa's declaration. If anything, his is being seen as emerging northern political agenda.

"Before now, something called the Babangida candidacy had gained currency. It was largely believed in some quarters that the former military president was warming up for an electoral battle with Obasanjo. The possible candidature of Babangida has since been placed on the weighing scale. But if there was any problem which analysts had placing a finger on Babangida's agenda, it is the present political arrangement in which power is ceded to the south. Nobody has said with certainty whether the north is prepared to retain the present arrangement for next year or have it tinkered with. Even those who take it for granted that the north would not field a candidate for next year's presidential elections are not certain whether the bloc would look eastwards for a presidential candidate. These have been issues for excited discourse.

"However, with the clarion call from northern governors which was actively backed and approved by the northern power elite, it does appear that the political coast is getting clearer. Bafarawa as the man of the moment has told the story of Nigeria's tomorrow as it appeals to the north. He minced no words in his declarations. Coming from an APP governor, it does not appear that the north has perfected a game plan to field a candidate for the 2003 presidential polls under the platform of the APP. This is especially so in the light of the fact that the new political associations are still awaiting registration.

"Another scenario which Bafarawa has brought to the fore is the primacy of the north west in northern political configuration. The zone, obviously the most disenchanted with the Obasanjo administration among the three geo-political zones of the north, is in a good position to pose a challenge to Obasanjo. Whereas the vice president comes from north east, a situation which might clip their wings to a reasonable extent, the same thing cannot be said of the zone that produced the Speaker of the House of Representatives whose relationship with the president has been anything but cordial.

"The story of the Middle Belt which dominates the north central zone is a different one. The Middle Belters seem to be caught in a crisis of identity. While some say they are not northerners, others prefer to say that they are northerners from the Middle Belt. Tendencies such as this have not helped the zone in taking a decisive position in matters that concern the north. Thus, if Obasanjo has any hold in the north at all, it can be said to lie in the north central zone.

"Given this state of affairs, it makes sense to see the north west leading the impending onslaught against Obasanjo. This is where the choice of Bafarawa makes the greatest sense. Whether it is by design or sheer coincidence, there must be something going for this governor who made such monumental declarations in the week the Sharia Court of Appeal in his state let off Safiya, the woman who was sentenced to death by stoning for adultery. Bafarawa has since upheld the judgment to the relief of all concerned. The Safiya case was a distraction. He did not need it. A more momentous project lies ahead- that of wresting power in the interest of the north.

"If all other weeks were to be like last week for Bafarawa, he would, sooner than later, become the cynosure of all eyes and the rallying point of the northern power elite. For Bafarawa, there may be many more rivers to cross, but at least, the journey has begun in earnest."[19]

Dawn of Democracy

These were my initial impressions of Bafarawa. When I met the governor again a couple of times in Sokoto and Abuja, I did not have cause to change my opinion of him. I still found him forthright and courageous. One of the earliest things that struck me about Bafarawa was his unpretentious disposition. He is a man of his words. He is a devout Muslim who believes in the tenets of the teachings of Prophet Mohammed. His devotion to doctrinal issues is total. I came to know this of him in 2002. By that year, re-election fever had put Nigeria on edge. Governors were campaigning for a second term. The Presidency was torn apart by Obasanjo's second term ambition as well as that of the Vice President, Atiku Abubakar. Second term was the sing-song across the country then.

Surprisingly, Bafarawa approached the issue differently. The good people of Sokoto State were beseeching him then. They wanted him to step out and declare for a second term. But Bafarawa would not be moved by that. Rather than join the second term train, he decided to give the people of the State an account of his stewardship.

In his address to the people as part of the activities marking the third anniversary of his administration, Bafarawa reminded his people that Allah gives power to whom He wills and takes it from whom He wills and that in His hands are all things. Having said this, he went ahead to remind the people that Islamic legislations forbid anybody to seek political power. He said:

"In fact, the Holy Prophet has made it categorically clear that power should be denied anybody who canvasses for it. Hence, it is the responsibility of the Ummah to nominate a person who by virtue of his qualities is considered capable of protecting the interest of all without fear or favour. I wish to state with all humility that it is on the basis of this consideration that I have remained mute over the Tazarce or Tamike trend that is being introduced in the country's political structure. It is important to remind all Muslims that Sharia is not just about stoning or caning or amputation of offenders. Sharia is all encompassing. In fact, it starts with us as leaders who should set examples for our subjects to follow. I cannot see myself who signed the Bill for the implementation of Sharia legal system into law turning round to flagrantly violate one of its cardinal principles, that is to say canvassing for power. If such a situation prevails, the ideals of leadership by example are certainly sacrificed on the altar of naked ambition. It may interest you to note that unlike in other state capitals, you cannot see posters of Tamike in Sokoto. The other day, some group of people staged a rally to the Government House chanting slogans of Tamike. I bluntly told them that the issue of Tamike does not arise. I further told them that they should address real issues that will propel good governance. In fact, I have tried not to fall into the Tamike trap. I would rather allow people to make that judgment instead of making Tamike my pet project at the expense of cogent programme of development that our state is in dire need of. Indeed, that is why I have today attempted to give the detailed account of my stewardship, telling my people how much we were able to generate, how much we spent and for what purpose. It is hoped that these accounts will guide the electorate in deciding whether it isTazarce or Talankwashe".[20]

This is Bafarawa, the quintessential man of principle and honour. Since I met this man, I have never had cause to sneer at him or his ways. He is truly dependable.

These avenging angels of democracy, as I have chosen to call them here, were no saints while in office. But they gave governance a refreshing and humane outlook. They did not give politics that ugly face of deceit and intrigue. They made it look like a decent human enterprise which it is supposed to be. Power was not a monster in their hands. Instead, they held it in trust for and in the service of the people.

Chapter 18

IN THE PURGATORY

I did not, by any chance, stumble into public office. My exposure to government circles was enough to earn me a place in the administration of some of the governors that I encountered.

However, by virtue of my nature and disposition, I do not hanker after anything. I operate with a self-sufficient spirit. Besides, I do not place value on people based on institutions they work for. I rate individuals based on their actual worth. Thus, in an environment like ours where people rush to play a role in government as if they are struggling to enter the Castle of Cinderella, I belong to the class of the contented ones who sneer and jeer at such beggarliness. Rather than join the amorphous crowd of job seekers in government circles, I prefer to sit back to reflect on the knowledge I have acquired in the academic field. I respect others like me who are thoroughly exposed to books and who place a higher premium on knowledge than anything else. For me therefore, the position anyone occupies in government does not matter. I am equally not moved by primitive wealth seekers who think that they belong simply on the basis of the fact that they have some disposable cash to toy with. I get amused when I encounter such misfits.

Owing to this disposition of mine, I have always allowed things to take their natural course. I have never really gone out of my way to seek recognition from anybody.

But my exposure would not let me be. It was for this reason that I was, at one point or the other, sought after by people in authority. But the return of democratic rule made this more pointed. The military had been hounded out by pro-democracy forces and the political space had been liberalized. New governments across the states had taken off and the prime movers were, at that point in time, interested in talents who would help their governments to stabilize. I was always looked up to in government circles as one of the brains that can make positive contributions therein.

The first that I came in contact with in this regard was Chief Achike Udenwa, the Governor of Imo State (1999- 2007). I had, in 2000, encountered the governor. I was in Owerri then to see my friend (now late), Chief Ogbonnaya Uche who was the Special Adviser to the Governor on Economic Affairs. OGB, as he was popularly known, had gone to see the governor one particular night and asked me to accompany him. We met with the governor in Government House where I had very useful interactions with him. I was later to articulate my meeting with him in an article entitled: "Conversation with Achike Udenwa", published in THISDAY of September 19, 2000. Aspects of it read:

"I have had three opportunities in the last 13 months to hold talks with Governor Achike Udenwa of Imo State. The first was in July last year when the man was barely two months old in office.

"Then, THISDAY had undertaken an extensive tour of the states of the federation with a view to getting a feel of the programmes of action which the governors had mapped out for their states. The overall aim of the project was to discover how much action or platitudes, as the case may be, that had gone into the campaign promises of the governors; and if `possible, use our reports to either jolt them into more action or out of complacency. Apart from Udenwa, I also held talks with the governors of Niger, Enugu, Rivers and Abia states for the purpose of the same project.

"The second opportunity presented itself when Udenwa visited THISDAY offices in Ikeja late last year. The occasion was not a dialogue between the governor and I, but I was one of the editors who had cause to ask Udenwa questions on his programmes in Imo State.

"The first encounter was not as revealing as I had expected. What I met was an Udenwa who was economical with words. He outlined his programmes quite all right, but he was not elaborate. In fact, it was tempting, given his short and brisk responses, to conclude that the man was yet to put his acts together.

"But I did not succumb to that temptation. Rather, I regarded Udenwa and his government as an open enterprise that would be put in a straitjacket at the appropriate time. I neither condemned nor approved. I merely bidded time.

"The second encounter was somewhat different. Then, Udenwa had actually undertaken some projects. There were expectations that certain things ought to have been done. Conclusions had also been reached in certain quarters that certain things had not been done right. The governor responded to all this. He also had cause to comment on some burning national issues of the time, including the raging storm between Chief Evan Enweren, the then President of the Senate, and his colleagues in the National Assembly. Here too, Udenwa's delivery was careful and calculated. There were no slips. There were no controversial statements. In fact, there was no sensation. The governor's performance was acceptable, yet, we were torn between understanding his kind of man and his approach to matters of public service.

"From these encounters, I was able to discern that Udenwa is not loud. He is not a show man. He has no grain of controversy in him. He also does not play to the gallery. These tendencies were largely reflected in the man's approach to electioneering campaigns. Then, not many gave him a chance. But he emerged victorious at the end of the day.

"Thus, when Udenwa settled down at Government House in Owerri, he brought the same reserve to bear on his administration. It is an approach which has left a yawning gap between what is done and what the non-participant observer knows. It is a style of governance which de-emphasizes publicity in preference for quiet action. However, this approach to governance did not serve Udenwa's purpose at the end of the first year. He did not receive accolades from the watchdogs. In fact, he was rated low on performance.

"So, what went wrong? My third chance to speak with the governor, and that was only three weeks ago, afforded both of us the opportunity to place all the cards on the table as we know them. It will hardly be expected that Udenwa's rating, done by whoever, and with whatever parameter, should be dismissed by his government as a non-issue. Indeed, the matter is viewed with concern in government circles.

"However, that is not to say that the government in Owerri believes it has not done well. In fact, many of the governor's aides would tell you that no governor under the present political dispensation has done better than Udenwa. The governor may not be as swift as his aides in his assessment of his government. But he believes in his heart of hearts that he is on the path of redemption.

"Indeed, Udenwa did promise to redeem Imo from stagnation and decay. After the solid foundation laid by the Sam Mbakwe administration for sound industrial and infrastructural development of the state, successive governments in Owerri, most of them military, did nothing to actualize the Mbakwe Marshal Plan. They even brought rot and decay with their maladministration. It is common knowledge that the Tanko Zubairu administration which Udenwa succeeded had a running battle with well meaning citizens of the state over its sluggish approach to governance.

"Udenwa promised to change all this. When we met in July last year, he outlined his areas of immediate attention. To realize them, he set up four review panels to review questionable employments, contracts and plot allocations undertaken by the Zubairu government. A staff audit panel was also set up for the state's Secondary Schools Management Board. The aim of the exercise, the governor said then, was to get the necessary facts that would enable the government take steps towards the development of the state without infringing on the fundamental rights of the people in accordance with the new democratic culture.To ensure a successful take-off as well, the government undertook the re-training and re-orientation of top Civil Servants in the state who are key players in the implementation of state policies and programmes.

"That was then. Three weeks ago, the governor pointed at concrete projects. He drew attention to the many road projects that his administration has embarked upon across the state. Others included the laying of pipes and extension of water to the Prefab and Aladinma Extension areas of Owerri; Computer Pilot Projects in secondary schools in the state; renovation of General Hospitals, reactivation of the Imo Broadcasting Service and the Imo Concorde Hotel, and so on. In fact, the governor reeled out a very long list of his achievements so far.

"I had cause to believe him. His government may not have taken off with the speed of Hercules, but it has been able to find its feet. All the government needs do now is to consolidate on its path of progress.Yet, the insularity of the government remains a source of concern. Why is very little known of the government's points of strength? Must one visit the Government House in Owerri to be able to know what the government is doing? This is the crux of the matter. Some of the governor's aides were wont to argue that government is not run on the pages of newspapers. They believe that Udenwa's achievements are there to speak for themselves.

"But there is a snag. No government thrives well in a state of obscurity. Government succeeds better when information is properly managed. Democracy is people-oriented. It recognizes the right of the citizenry to know. In fact, democracy survives better in an atmosphere of interaction and mutual education. This is where media relations comes in. A self-imposed isolation could be counter-productive. Udenwa's administration is caught in this web. I did tell this to His Excellency. He shared most of my views. In the same way, I believed him when he took time to explain his programmes to me.

"But the fact remains that government's successes need to be marketed. In the modern setting, a good product no longer sells itself. There has to be a conscious effort by manufacturers and advertisers to pillory the consuming public into viewing their product positively. That is why elementary Commerce teaches that it is costly to advertise but more costly not to do so. The government in Owerri owes itself a responsibility to let information flow."[21]

This was the product of my meeting with Udenwa. After this encounter, the governor came to recognize that he met with an expert in media affairs. That realization brought us closer. By January 2001, he invited me over to his office and told me that I would become his next Chief Press Secretary (CPS). The governor had just dissolved his Cabinet then. While I was with him, he sent for the then Secretary to the State Government (SSG), Nze I.M.O. Umunna, to join us. Umunna came over shortly afterwards and Udenwa told him what he had told me. The governor said that he would not make that appointment on the basis of sentiment; that he needed a thorough-bred professional to handle that bit for him. Nze Umunna made a few interjections. The governor then asked me to go and await further information on the matter.

In March, 2001, Udenwa reconstituted his cabinet and appointed a new CPS. My name did not feature in the appointment.

A few weeks later, the governor came to Lagos and sent for me. We met at Eko Hotel and Suites. The governor did not tell me what happened. He did not tell me why he could not keep to his promise. But he remembered, all the same, that he made such a promise. He said instead that he would want me to remain at THISDAY and be his eye and ear in the media. I did not subject the governor to any cross-examination. But I was amused at the THISDAY aspect because I had no control over the place. What if I get sacked? I asked silently. All the same, I took what he told me with equanimity of spirit.

Regardless of this slip, the governor and I maintained a close relationship. I could say that I worked for him at an unofficial level on media affairs. He was always there to talk to me. Until he left office in 2007, he maintained a level-headedness that is most uncommon in most public office holders.

Chapter 19

A DARK HORSE MARCHES IN

The exit of Achike Udenwa did not take me out of the political radar in Imo State. The succeeding administration still had cause to interface with me. But the succession battle that ushered in Udenwa's successor was somewhat intriguing.

On April 14, 2007, Governorship and House of Assembly Elections were held in virtually all the States of the Federation. Imo, my home State, was one of them. Whereas the results of the House of Assembly elections held in the State were upheld by the Independent National Electoral Commission (INEC), the electoral body cancelled that of the governorship election on grounds of substantial irregularities. Based on the cancellation, the commission fixed a fresh governorship election in the State for the 28th of April, 2007.

Within the two weeks that fresh governorship elections were to hold, Imo was on edge. The Peoples Democratic Party (PDP) had earlier disqualified an Ifeanyi Ararume who won the governorship primary elections and rejected him as its candidate. But the court compelled the party to have him fielded as the candidate. It was too late in the day for the party to contest the order of the court. It therefore accepted Ararume in principle but decided, in practical terms, to work for the candidate of another political party. This development led to high level horse-trading on the Imo political landscape. A lot of possible and impossible scenarios were thrown up. Permutations of all shades seized the day. Imo was in for an impromptu arrangement that must produce a governor in two weeks.

It was in the course of this horse-trading that the name, Ikedi Ohakim, strutted unto the scene. The man ran the election of April 14 under the banner of Progressive Peoples Alliance (PPA). No results were declared for that election. Thus, while Ararume was gearing up for a robust contest to neutralize a repeat of the inroad which Martin Agbaso, the candidate of the All Progressives Grand Alliance (APGA), made in the April 14 elections, the system largely represented by the outgoing PDP government of Achike Udenwa in the State, was rallying round a new person. This new candidate was Ikedi Ohakim.

As a frontline journalist and respected columnist whose endorsement of a candidate must be taken seriously, the case of Ohakim was brought to my attention. I knew Ohakim by reputation earlier. I recall that I met him in January 2004 at Government House, Umuahia. We exchanged numbers then but did not really communicate much.

When his governorship issue came up, I recalled our earlier interactions even though they were not intimate. But even at that, the Ohakim matter presented me with a dilemma. I usually shy away from writing on the politics of Imo State because I do not want to be labelled. Besides, a major ethical demand of the journalism profession is that you should leave out an issue if you have interest in it.

However, after due consideration, I stepped out of my shell and caused to be published on the back page of THE SUN articles that made no pretences about their support for Ohakim's candidature. I was to follow this up after Ohakim won the election in an article entitled: "Promises of a New Day" published in THE SUN of May 7, 2007. It reads in part:

"I am compelled by an uncommon circumstance to reflect publicly on the politics of my state, Imo. This circumstance is the emergence as the first citizen of the state, of someone who, in my opinion, approximates to the right calibre of man that should lead a state of the enlightened as Imo.

"Over the years, I had, as a matter of policy, shunned public commentary on the politics of my state because I did not want to put myself on the same pedestal with minions who by virtue of the fact that they hold public offices, have come to see themselves as factors that must be reckoned with in the scheme of things. Even though I find my aloofness justified, the tragedy of the situation is that mediocrities and jackals have had a free reign in Imo, thus slowing down the pace of a state that ought to have been on the fast lane.

"One of the ugly manifestations of this state of affairs is the arrested development that has been the lot of the state for so many years. Ideally, it will make good sense to challenge this state of affairs. But if you cannot stand cheap blackmail, the better part of honour would be to indulge them. Otherwise, they would make the world believe that you are belly aching over their lot because the opportunity you craved for was denied you. This will be in spite of the fact that you may never have even entertained the idea of being given a political appointment. It is the state of affairs that has alienated many from mainstream politics. This botherlessness has given room to the emergence of a cabal whose stock-in-trade is to see to the suppression of the bright and the best. Strictly speaking, Imo has, for the greater part of its existence as a state, gone to the field with its second eleven. In some instances, it has even fielded elements whose classification falls below the second eleven standard.

"But it does appear that this unflattering era has gone full circle. There is a development in the air which seeks to obliterate the state's grisly past. The recent emergence of Ikedi Ohakim as the governor-elect of the state seems to hold the touch to this newness or regeneration.

"I had said earlier that the circumstance that got me to go into this issue is an unusual one. Until last week, I had hardly batted an eyelid over the governorship tussle in Imo State. I was somewhat indifferent about who will emerge. This was because I saw my state, once again, tending towards revisionism and retrogression. I wanted to have a fill of someone whose mission was to accomplish a vision. I was not convinced that someone who will take my state out of Egypt would get the stamp of approval of those who have the privilege and prerogative to give us what we want or do not want. So I, as always, relapsed into cynical inaction.

"However, we are all witnesses to the uncanny turn of events. After all the jostling and power play, Imo has been handed over to a member of its Talented Tenth. This is a rear discovery; indeed a development which promises to put the state on the proper pedestal for emancipation and development.

"The development is one that has aroused me from my self-imposed slumber. It is a situation that has, for once, forced me to abandon my policy flag and step out in the open to sing a requiem for the old order and a welcome song for the new day that we have on our hands.

"If I understand my emotional make-up properly, I will say that I am not given to celebrating mediocrity or vanity. Rather, I treat them with scorn and disdain. But when I encounter merit or quality, I call it by its proper name. The new era that we are about to step into represented by Ikedi Ohakim seems to have quality and merit as its defining elements. This development excites me. This explains why I have abandoned my sanctuary of privateness and stepped into the public domain with issues around Imo politics. That is the reason I have decided to get interested in how the scenario is realized. My honest concern in this matter is to journey along with those who have the right endowment and temperament to make my state a reference point in the foreseeable future.

"But how did we get to where we are today? We are all familiar with the intrigues that killed the dreams of the octopus called the PDP. This is one party that has taken party politics to the gutters. The party is consumed by its own system that it bothers less about the human element in the democratic enterprise. That was why the party willfully brought down an Ifeanyi Ararume who won its ticket for governorship primary elections. Ararume worked so hard to get to where he got to before the primary elections. But some people thought it was right and convenient to dismantle him. But the good thing is that the man has put up a good fight. Because the party said it did not want him, it threw away the baby with the bath water.

"If I were Ararume, I would not begrudge the Progressive Peoples Alliance (PPA) for being the ultimate beneficiary of the in-fighting in PDP. He has already made his point by successfully engaging his party, the PDP, in a titanic legal battle. For him now, the better way to go is to work together with PPA for the greater glory of the state."[22]

The article was very well received by many that matter in the state going by the responses I got. Before then, I had met Ohakim as the governor-elect. In fact, I was in Owerri on 28th April when the rerun elections held. Ohakim was declared winner the next day by INEC. I put a call across to him on that day to congratulate him. I later met him that night in the company of my wife, Chinyere, in his suite at Concorde Hotel. We shared some ideas on government and governance. My wife and I left shortly after.

About a week or so later, I got a call from Ohakim inviting me over to Owerri to come and see him. But I was scheduled to leave for Sokoto the next day to see my friend, Alhaji Attahiru Bafarawa, who was rounding off his second term as the Governor of Sokoto State. I told Ohakim that I would see him later in the week. I actually gave him an exact date. I left for Sokoto as scheduled, met with Bafarawa and left. There was no flight out of Sokoto on the day that I was to leave. There were no regular flights in and out of Sokoto by 2007. To ensure that I kept my scheduled appointment with Ohakim, I headed to Abuja by road. I was scheduled to see Ohakim the very next day. I got into Abuja that day at about 9 pm. I caught a slight fever after the hectic journey. The next morning, I boarded the first flight from Abuja to Owerri. On landing at Owerri, I called Ohakim and he told me that he just left for Abuja. He asked me to wait for his return the next day. He instructed one Chikwen Onuoha to arrange for my accommodation at Concorde Hotel.

Ohakim returned to Owerri the next day and we met in his hotel room at Concorde. At the meeting, he said to me: "I will like to work with you". I thanked him for the offer but added quickly: "As commissioner or what?" He responded thus: "Something like that". I have always known that once an established journalist is brought into government, he is usually assigned a media or information portfolio. I was not averse to that. But I drew Ohakim's attention that day to the fact that I have other competences other than that of information. We had very frank discussions. He asked me to await further contacts and briefings on the matter. But as it turned out, I did not hear from him on the matter again. He constituted his cabinet a few months after and his government took off in earnest.

However, in August of that year, Ohakim and I met in Detroit, Michigan, USA. We were both in Detroit for that year's convention of the World Igbo Congress. Our meeting in Detroit afforded Ohakim the opportunity to talk to me about the matter. He explained to me that his hands were tied. He told me how godfathers and stakeholders in the state hijacked most of the appointments. He still promised to make good his promise. I reasoned with him and we left the matter at that. But there was no real contact or communication between us. I could only recall calling him sometime in 2008 to congratulate him over his victory at the Election Petition Tribunal sitting in Owerri where he had been dragged to by some of the candidates that he ran the election with. The tribunal had then affirmed him as the duly elected governor of Imo State. We did not speak again until January 5, 2009.

On the morning of that day, I was on my way to my office for the usual Management Committee meeting that held every Monday at 10 am. I was on the highway driving at a fairly top speed. I was somewhere between Gbagada and Anthony Village in Lagos when my telephone rang. I slowed down a little in order to take the call. I did not know who my caller was because no name registered against the number. When I picked the call and said hello, a voice hollered from the other end. "My name is Ikedi Ohakim". I responded thus: "Oh Your Excellency". No pleasantries. He delivered his message. It was short and direct. "I want you to join my government as Commissioner in the next one month. Do you want to give me your answer now or should I call back later?" To this I responded: "Your Excellency, we have been on this issue for sometime. If you are ready now, it is okay by me". He then told me that it was a done deal, that nobody could stop it this time around. He also said I should not tell anybody about it but asked me to prepare and await further information. I thanked him and he hung up. One month later, I was sworn in as the Honourable Commissioner for Information and Strategy in Imo State.

Chapter 20

AGE OF INNOCENCE

I went into government with a child-like mentality. I had, before my engagement, had what I considered open and frank discussions with Ohakim. Our relationship had been on the basis of mutual respect. I recognized that he set out to make a remarkable difference in government. He wanted to do everyday things in an uncommon way. But he was not going to achieve his objective if he cocooned himself in an island of isolation. He needed to extend his hands of fellowship to those he believed would help him to drive his vision for the state.

No doubt, the governor's appointments, in some cases, were influenced by political exigencies. It is right to do so in any political setting. But there were some others in which confidence and competence played pivotal roles. Mine was one of them. I shared the governor's ideals. I knew that his lofty dreams would be realized if those he believed in played positive roles in his government. This mindset accounted for my disposition towards him and his government. I came in with a lot of candour. I was as sincere as I could be. I did so because I trusted in the dreams and ideas we shared as the touchstone that would take the state and its people out of the woods. For me then, what came first was excellence in governance. The howl and hustle of politics must wait.

To ensure that I made the right mark, I immediately reprogrammed the Ministry of Information and Strategy where I was posted to. I drew a line between the conventional way of doing the job which resided in the ministry and the evolving but more challenging aspect of it - that of media relations.

In the modern world, the Media has acquired a lot of stature and influence to the extent that it now plays a major role in shaping the policies of government. As a media practitioner of many years standing, I knew how critical the media can be in the perception of government's actions or inactions. I was prepared to bring verve and uncommon accomplishments to this aspect of the job.

Ordinarily, I was excited at the idea of being involved in media management at official levels. I had, for well over a decade before my appointment into government, been involved in media relations. I enjoy the occasional controversies that come with the job. By nature, I am a lover of controversies. I cherish intellectual engagements and the debates they often engender. However, my involvement and interest in controversies is somewhat limited by personality. I do not talk much and this is borne out of the fact that I am selective in my audiences. I can suddenly become reticent, even aloof, once I find myself in the midst of people of little learning. I usually would leave them alone to entertain themselves in the best way they can. But I can be drawn out easily when I am challenged by intellectual and reasoned arguments. When this is the case, the aggressive publicist in me manifests.

My management of the Ministry of Information and Strategy and its affairs tended more towards this media disposition. I worked as if my office was an extension of the News Room. My Secretaries in the office had a hell of time adjusting to the schedules of this Honourable Commissioner who worked as if he was still subjected to the dictates of headlines and deadlines.

This was my primary preoccupation. It did not matter to me that I did not know a lot of people in government circles. On my arrival, many of the appointees had besieged me. They were never tired of introducing themselves to me whenever we met at official gatherings. But a good number of them were not happy that they had to introduce themselves to me over and over again, yet I did not know who they were. Apart from my fellow Commissioners, I had a hell of time knowing who the other people, especially in the rank of Special Advisers and Senior Special Assistants, were. This went on for a reasonable length of time until one of them, a Special Adviser, spoke angrily to me. The gentleman threatened that he would not talk to me again if I failed to recognize him the next time we met. I was later to find out in the course of my stay in government that the fellow in question was a Steve Asimobi who was then the Special Adviser to the Governor on Electoral Matters. With time, I got reasonably familiar with a lot of the appointees. But there were still a few that I could not identify with their names until we left government.

Chapter 21

THE HONEY MOON

The first six months I spent in government were fulfilling. I did my job without let or hindrance. I shared my media thoughts with the governor and he always supported them. Where funding was needed, I approached him and he readily approved. With the governor's support and cooperation, I carried out my responsibilities to the best of my abilities. My ultimate goal was to ensure that I did my best for his government. I was so committed to this objective that if anybody had told me at that time that my cordial and robust relationship with the governor was giving some people around him sleepless nights, I would have dismissed that as inconsequential given the fact that the governor and I were pursuing the same objective of giving his government a good name and a good image. This was in spite of the fact that I knew that such petty jealousies were part of an environment such as the one we were operating in.

I was also not ignorant of the fact that most people in positions of authority enjoy gossips around them. Gossip buoys their sense of security. It gives them the impression that there are lieutenants in their flock who are working hard to ensure that enemies within are exposed. Men of power and influence enjoy the presence of such hangers-on because tales from them give them updates on who is doing what around them. But the man of power who entertains such characters hardly takes into consideration the fact that the tale bearer's motive may not be altruistic; it may be sinister and therefore not in the best interest of the master. While some men of power may be circumspect in their dealings with such gossips, some others simply give them a free reign because their tales give them some kind of flagellation.

It becomes even easier for the gossip to have his way with the master when the object of gossip is made of a different stock. If he does not gossip as well to neutralize or counterbalance those of others, he becomes something of a lone ranger. When the same kind of story is told about him repeatedly before the man of power, then he (the man of power) begins to believe such stories. Indeed, Paul Joseph Goebbels, a Nazi German politician and Reich Minister of Propaganda of Nazi Germany from 1933 to 1945, tells us that " if you tell a lie big enough and keep repeating it, people will eventually come to believe it."23 This Goebbelian philosophy could, unfortunately, make the person being lied about vulnerable.

I was aware of such booby traps. But my confidence resided in the fact that I was not one stranger who was foisted on the governor by one godfather. I was the governor's creation, his nominee and appointee and his subject without question. On my part, I accepted this man as my master in government since I had no godfather anywhere. I would therefore not do anything that would go against the interest of this man who reposed confidence in me. So, I carried on unperturbed.

But it was not as if I did not get hints sometimes that government is a haven for intrigues and bad blood. About two weeks after I joined the Ohakim team, a strategic Retreat was held for members of the Expanded Executive Council at Nike Lake Resort, Enugu. While having a pep talk with Ethelbert Okere, the Governor's Special Adviser on Public Enlightenment and Documentary, I had asked him what the situation in our government was like. He said it was okay. But he advised me to try and do one thing. He said that I should, once in a while, go to the Chief of Staff of Government House to tell him what I was doing. I asked him why. He said: "Just to humour him". When he said this, I took a long, inquisitive look at him. "Just to humour him?" I muttered silently. "Why do I need to humour him?" I asked myself inwardly. I did not say anything to Ethelbert. I merely muttered a long-drawn "hmmmm". I did not inquire further into the matter. But I knew that I was not going to "humour" anybody, whatever that meant. It would run against the common grain of my character. But I did not commit that to heart. I forgot about that discussion and continued to discharge my responsibilities as diligently as I could.

I also did not bother about the fact that spoilsports could throw a spanner in the works. Even when it was mentioned to me that one or two members of the Governors' media team were doing unethical things, I did not make an issue out of it. The first hint I got in this regard was dropped by Chikwem Onuoha, the Governor's Special Adviser on Special Duties.

In September 2009, I had, in the company of Chikwen and Chuk Chukwuemeka, the Special Adviser on Economic Affairs to the Governor, travelled to Washington DC, the United States of America, for the Congressional Black Caucus Conference. That trip afforded Chikwen the opportunity to know a little more about me. Chikwen had noticed that I do not play hide and seek. He was convinced that my media interventions for the government were completely altruistic. He knew that I did not invent stories or cook up situations in order to extort money from the governor. Based on this knowledge, he thought that I should be put in the know about what some of my colleagues in the media team were doing. That was how he opened up to me. He told me that some of my colleagues write or cause to be written negative stories about the government and then go to the governor to collect money in order to counter such stories. He laughed roaringly in his usual manner as he made this revelation. Chikwen is always full of life and I took that to be part of the hilariousness he was known for. I heard him well enough, but I did not take it to heart. I was not perturbed because I felt that the governor was too wise to fall for such cheap antics. I chose to focus my attention instead on what took us to Washington DC. When we returned from that trip, I summarized my impressions in an article entitled "Ohakim: Home and Away", published in Saturday Champion of October 10, 2009. Aspects of it read:

"Already, it is an established fact that Imo State under the leadership of the present Governor, Chief Ikedi Ohakim, is a success story. The state in the past two years has become a model to be emulated. Ohakim has brought verve and vibrancy to bear on the governance of the state. The result is the unprecedented quantum leap that the state has witnessed in every index of human development.

"For the Nigerian audience, Ohakim's giant strides need not be over-emphasized any more. They speak for themselves. They are too obvious to be denied or repudiated even by the most virulent of his critics. But the situation is hardly the same on foreign shores. Even though we live in a world where information technology has broken down age-old communication barriers, the outside world cannot, by any stretch of the imagination, be expected to be as much at home with the goings-on in Nigeria as those of us that live and work here.

"Before now, Ohakim has had cause to tell the story of Imo state to the international community. But a significant difference was brought to bear on this when we visited the United States recently in the week marking the Annual Legislative Conference of the Congressional Black Caucus Foundation Inc. (CBCF). I was privileged to be on the governor's entourage. The governor featured prominently in the week-long event and this afforded him the opportunity to put Imo on the international wavelength.

"The CBCF, a non-profit, non-partisan, public policy, research and educational institute, aims at helping to improve the socio-economic circumstance of African-Americans and other underserved communities. Founded in Washington DC in 1976, it envisions a world in which the black community is free of all the disparities and able to contribute fully to advancing the common good. Its mission is to advance the global black community by developing leaders in forming policy and educating the public. It does this by facilitating the exchange of ideas and information. It was on the strength of this vision and mission of the CBCF that it outlined a number of fora and brain trusts during this year's conference to explicate and advance some of the issues that have been outlined.

"As a brand whose reach is fast going global, Ohakim was chosen by the CBCF to speak in one of the most important sessions, namely, the Energy Brain Trust, midwifed by Congresswoman Sheila Jackson-Lee. With the theme: "Where Do We Go From Here: Expanding Energy Opportunities Across the Globe", the session was put together by the constituency for Africa and the American Association of Blacks in Energy. Here, experts in energy and the environment came together at the Walter E. Washington Convention Centre, Washington DC, to share their thoughts and experiences on the global phenomenon. Ohakim featured on the panel that centred on green energy/alternative energy. Expectedly, he was at home with the issues. It was so principally because he has been involved in the issue of energy and environmental concerns. His state of Imo stands tall in the comity of states around the world that have taken the issues of environment and energy seriously. Here in Nigeria, Imo is amply recognized as an environment-friendly state.The Clean and Green Initiative of the

Ohakim administration has become the catchphrase in circles where the environment is discussed. And because we cannot really have a healthy and wealthy world without a clean environment, environmental concerns continue to play a prominent role in world affairs. The issues of global warming, ozone layer depletion, the ecosystem, aquamarine life and the like have become worldwide phenomena. Due recognition is therefore given to any individual, institution or government that pays attention to these all-important issues.

"For Ohakim, the session was a harvest of rare opportunities. Coming from Africa where the environment is freely and wantonly degraded, the American audience was delighted to note that there are leaders in the third world who have imbibed the civilized attitude that recognizes the centrality of clean environment in our quest to preserve our flora and fauna. Ohakim is one such leader and the global audience in Washington DC took more than a cursory notice of this.

"The Energy Forum and subsequently the Business Presentation at Patton Boggs, a unique law firm, provided Ohakim the ample opportunity to sell Imo, indeed Nigeria, to the world. In fact, anybody who was still in doubt about the importance and centrality of reclaiming our environment needed to be in Washington DC to see the attention devoted to this all-important aspect of our lives.

"At the Business Presentation at Patton Boggs, Ohakim could not but expand the frontiers of the discourse. Patton Boggs, a national leader in public policy, litigation and business law, is known for innovative legal solutions and deep, bipartisan roots in Washington's political arena. It forges relationships between government and business. Founded in 1962, the firm parades over 600 lawyers and professionals in nearly 40 areas of legal practice. Its clients come from Fortune 500. The firm operates with the legal maxim: "If the law is against you, try and change the law."

"It was on the strength of the firm's pedigree that a principal partner at Patton Boggs, Robert Horn, sought to improve the relationship between Nigeria and the United States. He regrets that Nigeria has not been well represented in the eyes of the world. Copious references were made to Nigeria's leadership challenges. Patton Boggs noted that it was the absence of proper relationship management, for instance, that led to Hillary Clinton's denunciation of Nigeria and its leadership when she visited the country recently in her capacity as the United States Secretary of State.

"To deal with the unsavoury situation, John Fox, another partner at Patton Boggs, noted that the firm was determined to improve relations between Nigeria and the United States. Even though the concerns of Patton Boggs about Nigeria were well received, Ohakim had his own story to tell. He regrets the poor economic and social relationship that exists between Nigeria and the United States. He notes, however, that the time has come for Nigeria to actualize itself.

"One of the surest ways of doing this, he noted, would be to enhance international cooperation and understanding between Nigeria and United States. This is necessary because Nigeria has opportunities which the Unites States can tap into. To fully domesticate his presentation, Ohakim took his audience to Imo State, the Eastern Heartland, where uncommon things are happening. The Ohakim administration in Imo is re-engineering the state. Massive infrastructural development is going on. The state is set to have its own Refinery and Petrochemical Plant, he said. It is putting together an international resort and conference centre that promises to attract tourists from all over the world. The state's agricultural potentials are enormous and need to be explored and exploited by willing international partners.

"He regrets, however, that America is not taking advantage of the opportunities that abound in Nigeria because of stereotypes.

Nigeria is unjustifiably made to look worse than it really is. America and, indeed, the entire world will be doing Nigeria a world of good if they can drop some of their stereotypes about Nigeria.

"The country, he said, certainly, has its drawback. But it needs to be properly understood and issues put in their proper perspective. But age-old prejudices about Nigeria have not allowed this to flower. Ohakim holds that Nigeria will overcome some of its disabilities if America supports the right calibre of leadership in Nigeria.

"Ohakim's campaign for a new Nigeria in Washington was all-embracing. The facilitators of Congressional Black Caucus conference had also scheduled to have the governor speak at the National Democratic Institute (NDI), also in Washington DC. There, Barrie Hofmann, Senior Advisor and Director for West and Central Africa of the NDI were regaled with the phenomenon called Ohakimism. As an organization that responds to worldwide quest for popular civic participation, open and competitive political systems and representative and accountable governments, NDI has taken interest in Nigeria's fledgling democracy. While we were in Washington, what seemed to bother Hofmann and his team was the seeming one-party status, which Nigeria is assuming. The institute sees this as an aberration, which Nigeria must be saved from.

"But here, Ohakim cleared the fog. He moved the institute away from theory to practical politics. Nigeria, strictly speaking, is not living under the shadow of one-party state. What is the case is that the polity is not driven by any form of ideology or belief. In the absence of this cardinal essence of politics, what drives the system in Nigeria is the quest for political power. Ohakim noted that in the Nigerian circumstance of today, it is the dominant political party that readily guarantees access to political power. This explains the apparent drift towards one-partism. But the trend is not one that should worry anybody. It is a phase which will come to pass.

"With all the issue fora and brain trusts, the stage was then set for the grand finale of the Congressional Black Caucus conference (CBC). The 39th edition, which held at the Walter E. Washington Convention Centre in Washington DC had as its theme "reinvest… rebuild…renew." The theme was apt not only for the Congressional Black Caucus but for all black people, wherever they may be. The theme poignantly reminds us of the conditions that led to the formation of the CBC on January 2, 1969.

"Thirty-nine years down the line, black activism in the United States has become an undeniable force, culminating in the emergence of the first African-American president of the United States in the November 2008 elections. Thus, at the Phoenix awards annual dinner, Barack Obama, the American president of black extraction, was on hand to address the mammoth crowd at the convention centre. This time, those of us on the governor's delegation didn't have to watch Obama, the 44th president of the United States, on celluloid. He was with us in flesh and blood. We could feel his electrifying presence. He stood with arresting gait and awe as he gesticulated from one end of the massive hall to another. Occasionally, the audience would rise with sporadic applause. The president was making sense. He was connecting meaningfully with the people.

"I sat side by side with my governor. As Obama took the American audience to emotional lows and highs, I imagined my governor taking his audience, as he normally does, into paroxysms of excitement. Ohakim certainly may not be an Obama in the American sense of it. But back here at home, he remains one of the most persuasive public speakers we have around. Thus, as Obama thrilled us in Washington DC, I knew that sooner or later, we would return to Nigeria to continue with the thriller from Ohakim. We are back and the exciting moments have resumed."[24]

This was my rendition of the trip. Those who read this piece at the time it was published in a number of Nigerian newspapers had no doubt that the writer believed in what he had written. There were no attempts at impressionism.

Before then, I had had occasion to demonstrate that I was a firm believer in the Ohakim project in government. On 23rd of March, 2009, Ohakim won an election petition case at the Court of Appeal, Port Harcourt Division. When judgment was delivered in his favour, the governor who was monitoring the court proceedings from his country home in Isiala Mbano ran out in excitement. The cameras captured him and his ecstatic mood. As the Commissioner-Reporter that I was, I wrote an article on the subject matter and circulated it to newspaper houses in Lagos. Aspects of the article entitled "New face of a Prometheus" published in SUNDAY SUN of March 29, 2009, read thus:

"You would think that he is a marathoner going by the quick dash he made immediately the Court of Appeal, Port Harcourt Division, pronounced him the indisputable winner of the April 28, 2007 governorship election in Imo State. But he is not. But the sartorial splash which his athletic appearance represents has continued to tickle the imagination of those who cherish the uncommon.

"Ikedi Ohakim, the Governor of Imo State, was in his sprightly best that radiant afternoon. The good news from Port Harcourt had unleashed a paroxysm of agreeable feelings in lovers of truth. But Ohakim stole the show when he broke loose from the restrictions of protocol. It took the watching lenses of a cameraman for Nigerians to be graced with the arresting aura that the Governor radiated on that fateful afternoon.

"That display by Ohakim has quickly reminded me of the submissions I made about his personality in some national newspapers between February 21 and 22, 2009. I had, in those publications, likened the Governor to the mythical Prometheus who stole fire from the gods and gave it to man. What this was supposed to mean is that Ohakim is a heroic explorer whose uncommon exploits are there for one and all to see and appreciate. This was precisely what he accomplished in Port Harcourt when he won the last of the epic legal battles that the opposition in Imo State has unleashed on him.

"I need not bother you with the details of the vacuous arguments and submissions which made nonsense of the case brought by Ifeanyi Ararume against Ohakim. Suffice it to say, however, that the case was roundly and squarely dismissed as incompetent, omnibus, hollow, baseless and generally laughable. What this means is that the case was founded on quicksand. That explains why it collapsed like a pack of cards.

"But we need not flog a dead horse. Rather, we should concern ourselves with what we must do to be in league with tomorrow. It is significant to point out that Ohakim, as a matter of fact, has not really been perturbed by the idle engagements of those who hate his presence in Government House Owerri. Rather, he engaged in a single-minded pursuit of good governance and all that appertain to it. He is a child of conviction who is hardly persuaded or impressed by the howling of the ignorant and the untutored. That is why he has chosen to trudge on like a Spartan instead of joining issues with intellectual lilliputs who can hardly appreciate the intricacies and complexities of governing a modern State especially in an environment as raucous as ours. It is because his brains are actively engaged with development issues that he cannot have room for the feather-brained.

"In the face of all of this, Ohakim has become the tiger whose head is sought after by weaklings who have taken to blackmail rather than take a direct shot at their target. Soon, his attackers would exhaust all the arsenal in their armoury. Then, the Promethean tiger would step forward in style and assume the role of a Romantic Hero who, by the sheer scope of his imagination, necessarily and compulsorily towers above his environment and his peers. It is just a matter of time."[25]

After reading this article, some of my colleagues in the media called me to comment on it. The impression the article gave them was that I was making my governor look like a super human specie of mankind. We laughed with a certain shared understanding and moved on to other issues.

Chapter 22

THE KALU-OHAKIM WEDGER

On 25th July, 2009, the then President of the Federal Republic of Nigeria, Alhaji Umaru Musa Yar'Adua, was in Imo State on a One-Day Working Visit. His visit was two-pronged. He was in Imo to commission some projects of the state government, notably the state-of-the-art Orient Television and Orient Radio studios and transmitters. He was also to formally receive Governor Ohakim who was returning to the Peoples Democratic Party (PDP) from the Progressive Peoples Alliance (PPA).

On that auspicious day, Yar'Adua commissioned the projects as scheduled and then retired to Dan Anyiam Stadium for Ohakim's reception ceremony. At the ceremony, Ohakim, naturally, had to explain why he returned to PDP. The reason d'être for his action was reassuring not only to the Imo electorate but also to well-meaning Imo PDP faithful. But the most telling statement people took away from the occasion that day came from the former president, Olusegun Obasanjo. He told the audience that Ohakim's return to the PDP was in keeping with his promise to come back to the party after his installation as governor. For Obasanjo therefore, the PDP family was happy that Ohakim had kept his promise and that the party had made a big catch in a serving governor.

But while PDP savoured its gain, someone was cringing at the development. Whatever that was PDP's gain was somebody's loss.

The PPA on whose ticket Ohakim rode to the governorship seat was not happy about the development. It felt betrayed by the action of the governor. In fact, the rumour about Ohakim's impending defection caused disquiet within the ranks of PPA.

But before the event took place, Imo was agog with expectations and reactions. Politicians commented freely on the impending defection, but their positions were largely shaped by their political leanings. One of the earliest comments came from Chief Arthur Nzeribe, a frontline Nigerian politician and chieftain of the PDP. In an article entitled "Ohakim's Return to PDP Will Heal Wounds" published in THISDAY of 21st July, 2009, Nzeribe held that Ohakim should return to the PDP, regardless of PPA's misgivings, because of the peculiarity of the Imo case. By the Imo case, Nzeribe was raising the question: "Who, between the PPA and PDP, really gave Ohakim the votes that brought him into office?" Nzeribe's answer was that it was the PDP that gave Ohakim the votes that made him governor. Based on this, Nzeribe asked again: "Of what benefit is it for the people of Imo state for the governor to remain in PPA when more than 90 percent of the people that voted for him are in PDP?"

But PPA had a counterpoise to Nzeribe's argument. It argued that it gave Ohakim the ticket that made it possible for him to contest as governor. Nzeribe then went further to dismiss this argument by holding that getting a ticket was an entirely different thing from getting the mandate. Nzeribe said:

"It is wrong for PPA to claim that Ohakim is holding its mandate because the party (PPA) did not have the population to give Ohakim the mandate. Agreed that the PPA was at the time of the April 2007 elections growing in popularity in the Igbo states of the South East, it had not yet gathered enough following to muster enough votes to singularly give its candidate victory. Ohakim's victory at the April 28, 2007 polls came essentially because the

PDP, for reasons already too well known to be repeated here, threw its weight behind Ohakim who was the PPA candidate. The PDP called out its members and supporters who constitute a far greater majority of voters in the state to vote for Ohakim instead of the official candidate of the party. And they complied. PPA alone couldn't have mustered the over 700,000 votes Ohakim got to place him well ahead of the fellow who took the second position…"

Nzeribe stretched his argument further. He said:

"How else would the PDP be expected to reap from what it did other than wanting to have the governor back to its fold? Since what we are talking about is struggle for power and not social clubbing, PDP is of course, right to have back a governor who has over 80 percent chances of being re-elected for a second term in 2011 on account of his performance so far. What else is politics? What is immoral about it? And what offence would Chief Ohakim be committing in looking for a platform that would make it easier for him to get re-elected in 2011 at least to complete his programme of massive transformation of the state?"

Nzeribe continued:

"It is in the overwhelming interest of the people of Imo State for Governor Ohakim to return to PDP. It will make for better stability of the Imo polity. As we have seen, it is by the sheer grace of God and good nature of some people that we have witnessed the type of harmonious relationship between the Imo Legislature and the executive arm of government personified by the governor. Ohakim is a wise man. Suppose tomorrow something comes on his head and he becomes power-drunk, who will mediate between him and a legislature which has only one member of his present party, the PPA?"

Nzeribe concluded his argument thus:

"PPA has the right to complain but there is a limit it can do so. It is wrong for its leaders to accuse the PDP of trying to reap where it did not sow or accuse Governor Ohakim of biting the finger that fed him. As we have seen, the party did not have what it takes to elect him all on its own. Even the fact that he (Governor Ohakim) has governed successfully for more than two years now is not entirely of its (PPA's) making. It is, as we have seen, as a result of the cooperation he has from PDP members many of whom have put partisan interest below the general interest of the people of the state".

This was Nzeribe's submission. But Ohakim's problem over the planned return to PDP did not rest with PPA alone. Even some elements within the Imo state wing of the PDP were opposed to his return to the party. There were people within the PDP in the state who felt that Ohakim's entry into the party would rob them of their privileged position in the party. To this end, they took steps to frustrate his return to the party.

For this category of people, Nzeribe had this to say.

"For those PDP faithful who do not like the idea of Governor Ohakim's return, their lot is to describe them as the worst enemies of the party and by extension the state. A party member who does not want an incumbent governor in his party should not be in partisan politics. He or she should remain in his household where he would remain the Alpha and Omega".

Nzeribe argued further that it was futile to stand against an Ohakim who had the power of incumbency. According to him, "Any member of the Imo PDP who believes that it would be easier for him to become governor in 2011 if and only if Ohakim does not return is being naïve and simplistic. For, in spite of the arguments in favour of his return, a simple peep into a scenario wherein Ohakim remains in PPA and decides to slug it out with the PDP would show that it would be a grand illusion to think that PDP can easily overrun him. Not in Nigeria can you overrun an incumbent governor just like that."[26]

The Kalu-Ohakim Wedger

This prognosis of the situation by Nzeribe prepared the ground for the debate that was to follow Ohakim's return to PDP, before and after it. While politicians analysed the situation from their partisan standpoints, commentators on national issues, particularly journalists, had their own views to express. This was the atmosphere and mood that pervaded the political space in the state. Yar'Adua and his entourage were through with the fanfare and had left. But what they left behind was the bitterness and acrimony that was to follow.

Somebody was bound to fire the first salvo. It came from Orji Uzor Kalu, the leader of the PPA. Kalu saw ingratitude in the action of Ohakim. He accused the governor of betrayal and of biting the finger that fed him. He said he did not expect such treatment from a man he said he had been taking care of for virtually all his life. He told the story of his long-standing relationship with Ohakim and denounced him for abandoning a friend who used the instrumentality of his party to make him governor.

But the missile from Kalu would not go unchallenged. Ohakim was bound to tell his own story. There was the need for him to set the records straight so that posterity would not be unkind to him. In his response, Ohakim held that Kalu lied against him. He then took steps to refute most of Kalu's submissions. The two big wigs told their stories in the open. They opened many can of worms. It was then time for the public to feast on the story. A great debate ensued. Commentators put Kalu and Ohakim on the scale and did whatever they liked with them.

Sam Omatseye of The Nation Newspaper described Ohakim's action as brave and pragmatic. It was, for him, real politick in action. He said Ohakim needed to make that move to stay afloat as governor "or else Imo could turn into Anambra of yore."[27]

Chiemeka Iwuoha of Champion Newspapers did not see any need for the hue and cry over Ohakim's return to PDP. He said what the governor did "was simply to align with political realities…to secure electoral victory". For him, "the dissenting and hysterical voices was just the case of leaking kettles calling corrugated pots black".

Chiemeka continued: "Within the subsisting electoral laws of the land where all things are not equal, Ohakim's chance, if the Imo state governor aims at or even wishes to seek re-election, would be vastly improved by joining the ruling party which controls the lawmakers of his domain."[28]

Achilleus Uchegbu also of Champion Newspapers, averred that Ohakim, having moved from the PPA to the PDP and having reflected on his journey and where Imo people want the state to be in the next few years, acted wisely. For him, Ohakim "took the best decision in the interest of Imo state. I am not sure Imo people were or are willing to be tied to the aprons of PPA which future, emanating from organizational inadequacies, is suspect."[29]

Like other commentators before him, Luke Okoro of Champion Newspapers did not disapprove of Ohakim's action. He said the governor left PPA to join a party "where his return ticket is guaranteed, whether he performed well or not." As a serving governor who would want to return for a second term, Okoro held that it was obvious that PPA would not help Ohakim to realise that objective. Besides, since the leadership of the PPA had, some months earlier, announced that there would not be any automatic ticket for elected public office holders within its fold, Okoro submitted that "it would be foolhardy to think that Ohakim would want to, again go cap in hand, begging Kalu for a ticket."[30]

For Godwin Nzeakah, Ohakim's decision to return to PDP was a courageous one. He described the move as "a classic demonstration of courage and ability to appreciate the signs of the times and the mood of the critical, if controversial majority, in his domain". He further saw it as an effort to forestall tension within the constitutional framework and try to "explore new frontiers, new possibilities, peacefully, while simultaneously consolidating previous gains in the quest for advancement, political stability and sustainable progress in Imo state."[31]

Muyiwa Daniel also approves of Ohakim's action. He said the governor was proving that "governance is a pledge made to people and which must be fulfilled, not satisfying the whims and caprices of meddlesome godfathers who, in reality, don't deserve being described as democrats."[32]

Nnamdi Nwosu described Kalu's rage against Ohakim as unmerited. He said that it was "the height of hypocrisy if Kalu insists on shutting Ohakim up while he himself is free to do what he likes on the political terrain". He then raised the question: "if Kalu could quit PDP the way he did, he should not begrudge Ohakim a similar right to quit the PPA within the law without being victimized or demonized". He then submitted that Ohakim's decision to go back to PDP was in accord with the provisions of the 1999 constitution of Nigeria which guarantees freedom of association.[33]

In the face of these commentaries most of which were in support of Ohakim's action, Kalu's media goons picked up the gauntlet and freely used their platforms in THE SUN to fight their master's war. On their part, Ohakim's media team took up the challenge. Their Governor cannot be run over just like that while they watched. They joined the fray and the controversy raged.

The situation presented me with a dilemma. I stood the risk of being the fall guy of the controversy. Kalu was my boss at THE SUN. I had left the newspaper less than five months from that time to work for the Ohakim administration. I could therefore not bring myself to antagonise my employer. He was, indeed, still my employer because I did not resign from the newspaper before joining Government. I was only on leave of absence. Even if I had resigned, that would not give me the liberty to go to war with a former boss whom I had no problem with. But I would not stay out of the controversy completely. Therefore, after weeks of the media war, I opted for the middle-of-the-road approach and interjected as follows in an article entitled: "The Great Debate over Ohakim" published in Daily Champion of August 17, 2009. It partly reads:

" I have followed with keen interest the debate that has been sparked off by the return of Chief Ikedi Ohakim, the Governor of Imo State, to the Peoples Democratic Party (PDP). My interest in the matter is understandable. Apart from the fact that I am an established commentator on national and international affairs, the man at the centre of the storm is my governor and my boss. Besides, Chief Orji Uzor Kalu, the man whose party is aggrieved over Ohakim's action, is also my boss. Quite a number of people feel that this situation presents me with a dilemma.

Ordinarily, it would seem as if I am caught between two stools. But I do not, strictly speaking, think so. This is because the issue at stake, when divested of all its pugnacious connotations, will come alive as a public affair which I still remain entitled to comment on. I will therefore proceed on the strength of the assumption that I reserve the right to be heard on this or any other issue for that matter regardless of my affiliation with Ohakim and Kalu. Besides, if we must appreciate the issue for what it is, we must see Ohakim not as the issue but as an affected Nigerian and party man whose action is being used as a case study in the ongoing debate.

"I use the word 'debate' advisedly here. This is because a good number of the people who have taken interest in the matter and who have commented publicly on it did not follow the basic rule of debate which requires that you must have a point of view and demonstrate why and how your point of view is superior to that of your opponent. It is this basic requirement that draws debate or arguments to the realm of logic. Any argument that is based on logic must follow the rule of syllogism which in itself requires that conclusions reached in an argument must be deduced from the propositions which form the raw material of any argument.

"It is regrettable that this requirement which is intrinsic and proper in the art of reasoning has been violently ignored by many a commentator on this issue. What some of them have done instead is to freely insult and abuse. They are directed at the personalities involved. By so doing, they fail to do justice to the dialectics of defection. They have also erroneously treated the object as the subject. This misplaced form of argument commits the ad hominem fallacy in logic.

"The debate, no doubt, was sparked off by the misgivings which the PPA expressed over the exit of Ohakim from the party. Considering the fact that Kalu is the founding father of the party, those who have sympathy for him flew off the handle without subjecting the issue at stake to reason and commonsense apparently because they felt that Kalu was decidedly against Ohakim's action. This bangwagon mentality has been largely responsible for the uninformed and jejune commentaries on the issue. But it is reassuring that Kalu himself took a frontal position on the issue. Contrary to the howling of many who thought they were fighting his cause, Kalu has said that he is not really perturbed by Ohakim's change of platform. He said his grouse rests largely on the governor's complaints to the Department of State Service which led to Kalu's invitation and interrogation by them. Kalu has, by this declaration, taken the wind off the sail of the uncritical minds that have packaged and sold Ohakim as a villain without recourse to reason or even commonsense.

"Then you ask: why the rash of hollow commentaries on the action of one man? The answer is not far to seek. In a setting such as ours where people hardly task their mentality, what reigns supreme is mediocrity. With such a mindset, defection must be bad because somebody who is a member of the ruling party has said so. Thus, without subjecting the issue to the rigours of analysis or ratiocination, the untutored minds who pose as commentators go to town to celebrate their ignorance, prejudices and biases. Once any debate is visited by these negative tendencies, reason no longer serves any purpose. It becomes a tool which exists for its own sake.

"But it is hardly surprising that controversy is raging over Ohakim's action. In fact, it will not be out of place to say that the political life of Ikedi Ohakim, beginning from May 2007 when he assumed office as governor, until now, has become synonymous with controversy. The man took the centre stage of Imo politics rather dramatically. Ever since, his actions and even inactions, have been defined by the unusual. In all of this, it would appear that the controversies have largely been sustained by the convictions and doggedness of the man who has been at the centre of the morass. Indeed, the received notion is that most of the people who have been engaging the governor in bitter and acrimonious political wars would have beaten some retreat were Ohakim not as stubborn as he has proved to be. But if we proceed on the assumption that the governor is tenacious, then it would make a lot of sense for us to inquire into this unusual approach to public affairs.

"The real bone of contention this time borders on the well-worn decision of the governor to return to the PDP from whence he joined the Progressive Peoples Alliance (PPA). Perhaps the on-going attrition over the governor's return to PDP would have been averted were he lily-livered about the issue at stake.

Prior to his return, it was evident that certain elements would not be properly disposed to the development. The expectation in certain circles then was that the governor should not throw his hat into the ring. He was harangued, cajoled and even blackmailed into retracing his political steps along the line of change of platform.

But such moves proved ineffective because they were founded on a poor understanding of the essence of the man in question. If only they knew that the essential Ohakim does not suffer fools gladly, they would have saved themselves the restlessness that underlines their apprehension. The truth is that the governor is not swayed by the opinion of the anonymous public. Like a Romantic Hero, his imagination usually towers above that of his immediate environment. The result is that many around him sometimes cannot come to terms with his method. But at all times, he has a reason which, more often than not, does not conform to the untutored mentality of the common herd that populate our political space. It is because he weighs his actions properly and looks very well before he leaps that he does not easily get swayed to the side of the contrary when he is on the move. It is this pursuit of reason and conviction based on properly weighed and balanced options that some describe as stubbornness. But those who understand this essential make-up of the man have since come to appreciate the fact that Ikedi Ohakim's approach to matters of conviction is what a system needs to identify and edify itself.

"The need to hold on to one's cherished values becomes even more paramount in the face of the quality of people that strut in and out of our civic space. It is regrettable that Nigeria remains the haven of turncoats and upstarts who see politics as the business for one and all. That is why minions and questionable characters invade the political space and expect decent men and women to pander to their reprehensible whims and caprices. It is situations such as this that give rise to the stubbornness of the Ikedi Ohakim variety. It is this predisposition that gave him all the courage and valour with which he fought all the legal battles that came his way. While many thought that he should negotiate with his detractors, he dared them in the legal combat in a manner that left many of them gaping. Somehow, he has weathered the storm and many have come to appreciate the fact that the law courts are a good place to be once you are convinced that you are on the right track.

"Now, what is the issue at stake? Why is a brand new controversy being woven around Ohakim? We are being made to believe by some that Ohakim has erred by returning to PDP. The PPA, the party he left, has been particularly irked by the governor's action. No doubt, PPA has every right to feel aggrieved. It is not a good development for a political party, especially a budding one such as PPA, to lose a foundation member and a vibrant one at that. For the party, the loss of Ohakim will deal a devastating blow to its fortunes. Its perception in the eyes of the public will even plummet. But rather than the hue and cry over the loss of Ohakim, PPA should work towards protecting its frontiers. It should begin to adopt an approach that will make it unattractive for its flanks to be invaded. Above all, the party has to strive to deal with the problem of integration so as to escape the threat of disintegration.

"Beyond the bad blood over the loss of Ohakim, the PPA will be making a better impact in the years ahead if it pays less attention to the loss of one man. Changing political platforms, for whatever reason, is an integral aspect of politics the world over. At a certain time in the political career of a politician, situations that demand a change in platform do arise. When they do, politicians use their judgment to know when and how to flow with the tide. This is what Ohakim has done. It is legitimate in politics. Many have done it before him. Many will still do it after him. To treat Ohakim's case as a special event is a way of saying that there is something peculiar about everything the man does. Is Ohakim an enigma whose actions are beyond comprehension? Why does his name excite the polity to the point of frenzy? Attempts at answering these questions, I believe, will deepen our hold on the Ikedi Ohakim phenomenon.

"As we wait for time to give us more insight into what experts in coinages would call Ohakimism, I must say that I have never been swayed by arguments which tend to give the impression that there is something wrong with changing political platform. That is why I will not pay attention to the stories of defection or change of platform that democracies around the world, including the United States, are replete with. We can only go into such discourse when it becomes an issue. For now, I believe that we are being entertained by those who cannot come to terms with the action of one man.

"But what I find most amusing about the entire drama is the puerile reference that is being made to morality. By that I mean that some people are saying that Ohakim has committed a sin by changing political platform. I do not think that I have really encountered any sound mind who made allusions to that. What I have seen instead are the declarations and submissions of tainted souls whose stock-in-trade is to regurgitate arguments or viewpoints that they cannot even properly espouse, let alone defend. If anybody of note had made an issue of this, we will begin to retort by taking just a cursory look at the fellow's moral standpoint. If such a one survives the casual scrutiny, we will then face the round table and trash out the issues that may arise from the moral question. But since nobody has stepped forward to be counted in this regard, we will ignore the murmurs and howling on this aspect of the debate.

"But after the national feast that Ohakim's movement has become, we cannot but pay attention to the people of Imo State who really should be most concerned about what their governor has done. Since we occupy a vantage position in this matter, we are privileged to know that the issue for Imo people hardly has anything to do with belongingness to a political party. Rather, it is about the programmes and projects of the government of Ohakim.

Regardless of the party the governor belongs to, the people are not planning to forget or ignore the glorious impact the government has made and is still making in their lives. This is the issue, not the bad blood and the moral sanctimoniousness that is being inflicted on our psyche by pretenders to the slippery throne of morality and propriety."[34]

This was my submission on the matter. Then, after some more weeks of confrontation, the combatants burnt themselves out. The debate abated and then fizzled out.

In my own reckoning, I tried my best in managing the situation. But I did not know how the protagonists perceived me. I did not know what they thought I did or failed to do. Regardless of that, I continued to enjoy my relationship with the governor. There was hardly any week he did not invite me over to his office for us to discuss some issues confronting our government.

In September of that same year, just a day before I was to leave for the United States for the Congressional Black Caucus conference, the governor had reason to send me to Igbere, Abia State, to deliver a condolence message to Mr. Dimgba Igwe, the then Deputy Managing Director of THE SUN, who lost his mother. I was to be at the funeral ceremony but it coincided with the day I was to leave for the United States. Consequently, I had to visit Dimgba a day earlier to deliver the governor's message to him. While we were exchanging pleasantries, Dimgba asked me what my relationship with the governor was like. I told him that it was cordial. He said I was lucky. But he did not lose sight of the fact that Kalu and Ohakim had just ended a bitter quarrel. He then said: "One day, they will ask you to attack Kalu". At this, I had a good laugh and told him that that was not possible. Of course, I was never asked by anybody to attack Kalu and I never did.

Chapter 23

THE LULL BEGINS

The month of October 2009 marked the beginning of a new phase in my job as Commissioner for Information and Strategy. By this time, the funding of media activities by the governor had dropped. But that was not obvious to me at first. However, after some time, it became clear to me that some lull had set in. But I did not understand why. Up till that time as well, I had thought that every mail sent to the governor must necessarily get to him. But I was to realize otherwise when I wrote him while he was overseas. I was seeking a certain approval on behalf of the ministry. I was well aware that the governor was outside the country when I sent in my mail. My aim was to have the letter wait for him on his table so that he would deal with it as soon as he returned. Surprisingly, the mail was replied to less than four days after it got to Government House. The response did not meet my expectation. It was then that I realized that a governor could only see letters or mails that his principal staff members want him to see. It then dawned on me that the governor may not have seen some of the proposals that I sent to him that needed urgent attention. I had resorted to memo-writing when my access to the governor suddenly dropped. In the absence of face-to-face contact, I had to reach the governor through some other means. But little did I know that my mails may not have reached their desired destination.

Within the period of lull, my access to the governor reduced. He sent for me less often. But then, I did not feel that anything was the matter. However, I noticed once in a while that certain statements were issued in the name of the government without reference to my office. They usually appeared under the banner of "Government of Imo State, Office of the Governor." When I tried to query the action, I was told that it was the Office of the Governor, not the Government of Imo State, that issued the statement. I was told that my purview covered the Government of Imo State, not the Office of the Governor. The distinction was clearly nebulous and laughable to me. But I did not make an issue out of it. However, what was clear to me was that another layer of the Media Team had emerged. Information management had started flowing from diverse sources.

This went on for some time. Then one day, the governor invited me over to his office. I do not remember what the meeting was really about. But while I was with him, the Chief of Staff came in. Ethelbert Okere also joined shortly after. There was also one other person whom I am unable to remember. When Okere came in, he was clutching a publication in one of the day's newspapers. In it, one unknown, perhaps non-existent, organization had taken up a full page advertorial condemning the State Government over one thing or the other. Okere brandished it saying: "Your Excellency, we have to respond to this publication immediately." I collected the newspaper from him, glanced through the publication and then asked him "Who are you responding to?"

I argued that the organization was unknown. I pointed out that it was wrong for Government to take up every issue raised against it. I counseled that some of such publications should be ignored especially if they were coming from unknown and even non-existent sources. I said that Government would reduce itself to a laughing stock if it insisted on joining issues with everybody over everything, serious or unserious. I went further to say that

I did not understand the indecent haste even if Government had to respond. "How can a publication come out today and you have a response to it in the newspaper of the next day?" I queried. I held that if Government must respond, there was the need to look at the issues involved in a reasoned manner rather than rush out with an ill-digested, puerile response.

The Governor listened to me patiently. He acknowledged that I had a good point. But he said that we must, all the same, respond to anything and everything. He said such responses were necessary for the sake of posterity. According to him, if in the next 100 years someone reads what has been written about our government without a corresponding response from the government, it would be taken to mean that such a government is guilty as charged. I made concessions to him on the issue but insisted that we should not respond to that particular one from Okere because the organization in question could be fictitious and therefore does not deserve the attention of Government. At the end of our deliberations, the governor overruled me and the response written by Okere appeared in the same newspaper the next day under the banner of "Office of the Governor".

Developments such as this did not help the media direction of the government. They were recipe for confusion. The incident brought home to me what Chikwem had told me some months earlier in Washington DC. Going by the way it all went, it was not out of place to assume that the negative publication as well as its response came from the same source. The ugly development effectively set the tone for the image crisis that was to rock the government shortly afterwards.

In the face of this development, I began to develop a cold feet on media matters. Yet, I could not but face the task of ensuring that the actions of government were not twisted towards unintended ends by mischief makers.

In all of this, it was evident that the governor had been fed with half-truths and absolute falsehood about me. But it was difficult for him to swallow such gossips hook, line and sinker. He was torn between accepting my approach to media issues and going the way of the new-fangled, emergency media zealots who were bent on wresting the control of government's media activities from "the arrogant, all-knowing Dr. Amanze Obi".

Chapter 24

THE LAST STRAW

Regardless of the wedge that had been put in the information wheel of the government by the governor's emergency, self-serving devotees, I worked hard enough to maintain my sense of proportion. The situation did not get out of hand until 12th March, 2010 during the 3rd Enlarged Executive Council Policy and Strategy Retreat organized for members of the Expanded Executive Council at Amber Tinapa Hotel, Tinapa Resort, Calabar. At the retreat, someone from outside the government was commissioned as a resource person to make a presentation on media relations. There were also other resource persons who spoke on different aspects of government matters. I knew virtually all the resource persons. I had worked with some of them in Lagos and they had tremendous respect for me. Some of them were people who would come to me to ask for my opinion or position on any matter before they commit themselves to any position. Unfortunately, once you are in government, your expertise is usually taken for granted. You are seen more as a servant of the governor than as an expert. The outsider who has come to render consultancy services to the government you serve is automatically rated higher than you even though such a consultant may not measure up to you in real terms.

As a member of the government, I was on the side of the harassed audience that must listen to "experts" from the other side. And so, when this media man made his presentation, he made it appear as if information management has a formula. His presentation was a pot-pouri of prescriptions and proscriptions on media matters. As a matter of rule, we on the side of government were not allowed to argue or join issues with the "experts" who have come to "lecture" us. We were simply expected to absorb them and go home and do better in our various areas of assignment.

With about one year to the 2011 general elections, some of the presentations unsettled the governor somewhat. The media bit probably reminded him of our earlier disagreements over media and information management. Those who erroneously think that there is a hard and fast rule about media matters had fouled the air. The governor began to entertain the strange feeling, probably, that the expertise of his supposed in-house media guru who poses as an omniscient deity and shoots down any idea that did not emanate from him had been challenged or even weakened by the presentation from the outsider. He began to complain from the podium, almost involuntarily, that "When Okere says this, they will say it is wrong. When Okere says that, they will say it should not be done that way". Then he added for effect. "When you think that you are an expert, you will not know your limitations until you come in contact with other people."

That was the bombshell from the governor. There was disdain in his voice. I was stupefied by what had just transpired. The import of his remarks was probably lost on many members of the Expanded Executive Council. But its impact registered on me immediately. It was a direct reference to the disagreement we had recently in his office over what to publish and what not to publish. The governor had finally stepped out to denounce what appeared to him to be my overbearing and all-knowing disposition to media matters. I cringed at the point blank denunciation. I regretted that the governor, my confidante, had joined the mischievous mob who wanted me crucified. I had to give up. And I gave up.

When we returned from Tinapa, I invited the Permanent Secretary of the Ministry of Information and Strategy, Mr Justin Amafili, over to my office and told him that I was on my way out of the ministry. He asked why. He was at the Retreat. So, all I needed do was to refresh his memory. He said he was surprised at the way the governor spoke. Even Mr. Okere, the beneficiary of the governor's angry interjection, met me in front of the Multi Purpose Hall, Government House on the day we returned from the Retreat and told me that he was surprised at the way "Oga" spoke. I simply muttered a muffled mmmhhh and we went our separate ways.

Based on what transpired at Tinapa, I looked back painfully and reviewed my media activities for the government. I came to the conclusion that my efforts were not appreciated; that the governor probably never read any of my media interventions for him and his government. Or that he took them for granted, if he did. Consequently, I decided that I would no longer take interest in government's media activities. I decided to, thenceforth, concentrate on the conventional job of the Information Commissioner at the Ministry while waiting for my removal to be announced. Yes, I anticipated my removal and I wanted it to come fast.

With my quiet withdrawal from government's media activities, those who had been blackmailing me had a field day. They began to gossip that I no longer came to Government House to talk about media issues. They began to give the impression that I had abdicated my responsibility. Sooner than later, it became obvious to Government House that I had moved out of government's media radar. Yes, I had decided that I would no longer take interest in government's media matters. My withdrawal was obvious to all concerned but nobody had the courage to take up the issue with me. So, we just ambled along in that state of dumbness.

Within the intervening period, something that was supposed to draw me out from my self-imposed hibernation happened. The News Magazine had, in its edition of 5th April, 2010, carried a very negative cover story on Governor Ohakim with the unflattering caption "Brutal Ohakim: A Governor and His Many Scandals". The coming story was, as is usually the case with most weekly magazines, promoted in some weekend newspapers to whet the readers' appetite before the magazine would hit the newsstands on Monday. Government House was unsettled by the coming story. Something had to be done. Still, nobody dared call me to discuss it. Strangely, it was the Governor's wife that called me. She asked me if I was aware of the story The News magazine was coming up with. I told her that I had seen the promo. She asked me what I was doing about it. I told her that the Media Council would take a decision on the matter. She suggested a possible mop-up of the magazine. I told her that it would not help matters. Apparently not satisfied with my responses, she said: "Well, I am waiting for you and the media council or whatever you call yourself to see what you will do". I thanked her for her interest in the matter and she hung up.

I did not know what Government House did or did not do before the magazine appeared on Monday. But the copies were reported to be scarce in Owerri. A day or so after the publication appeared, Pini Jason Onyegbaduo (may his soul rest in peace), who was also a member of the Media Council, called to ask me if I was planning a response to the story. I told him that I was not. He said there was no need for a reply as that could open more avenues for further attacks on the governor. We left it at that.

The entire experience left a bitter taste in the mouth. Regardless of the inward pains, I remained in the ministry to lick my wound waiting for the inevitable. It was not until May that the governor reshuffled his cabinet.

On the day the governor was to effect the cabinet changes, the Executive Council meeting, as was the case on most occasions, extended into the early hours of the next day. Before our meeting commenced on that day, I got hints that "something was going to happen". And so, I monitored the governor's body language at the meeting that day. When the meeting was about to end way beyond midnight, he started talking about continuity and the need for him to continue to work with all of us. While he was making those remarks, I knew where he was headed. When he finally hit the nail on the head, he pushed a piece of paper to the Secretary to the State Government to read out the details of the reconstituted cabinet. My name was the first on the list. I had been moved to the Ministry of Culture and Tourism. Others who were affected in the reshuffle were probably taken unawares. But I was not. For me, the development was a conclusion long forgone.

Under normal circumstances, my redeployment was not supposed to be an issue. In fact, change of portfolios is normal in government. It takes place from time to time. Appointing officers, be they presidents, governors or any other person in position of authority, employ it as a means of giving a new lease of life to an administration or institution. Ordinarily, redeployment is supposed to be a well-worn tool in the hands of any administrator who desires to keep the engine of his administration constantly fresh. However, when it is employed as a punitive tool, its outcome, more often than not, becomes counter-productive.

As I said earlier, my redeployment was not supposed to be an issue. The governor had, prior to my appointment in January 2009, told me that he would redeploy me to the Ministry of Culture and Tourism after my tour of duty at the Ministry of Information and Strategy. He had his reasons which ultimately were tailored towards the good of the administration, and I had no problem with that. Unfortunately, when it was to take place, politics of bad blood was introduced into it, thus making a well-intended action look like a punitive one. But it was even possible that the governor, owing to the pressure he faced, may have forgotten at the time of his action, that his original plan was to move me from the Ministry of Information and Strategy to that of Culture and Tourism in due course.

However, whatever the reason behind the action was, the redeployment was supposed to officially bring to an end my involvement in the media activities of government. But it did not. The governor, after my redeployment, still sought my input and intervention in critical media activities of the government.

Chapter 25

AFTER THE FALL

After my fall from Olympian Heights as my detractors perceived it, the governor, in his quiet moments, probably felt the need to assuage whatever ill feelings that I might have. Thus, six days after the redeployment, he invited me over to his office and told me the reason for his action. He said he redeployed me to the Ministry of Culture and Tourism because he planned to use the remaining one year of his tenure to work on the Imo Wonderlake Resort and Conference Centre at Oguta. He said his plan was to have me beam media searchlight on the project. He said he knew that I was the only one around who has what it takes to engage in such an ambitious media activity. I noted what he said, but I took it with a pinch of salt.

At that meeting in his office, which had in attendance the Chief of Staff, Emma Ohakim; the Economic Adviser to the Governor, Chuk Chukwuemeka and the Director General of Imo State Investment Promotion Agency, Mr Chinedu Okpareke, the governor told me that I should assume the Chairmanship of the Committee on the Ground-breaking ceremony of the Wonderlake project. Chinedu was to be a member. Some other members were to be co-opted in due course. Before we rose from the meeting, the governor said to me: "I have told you now. Don't say I didn't tell you. Take charge."

That was the governor's verbal declaration. But I knew that appointment of Executive Council Committee members usually follows a pattern. Those appointed into committees are communicated officially in writing by the Principal Secretary to the Governor with clearly defined Terms of Reference. There was no such thing in this case. It looked to me like a strange way of assuming the chairmanship of a committee. However, regardless of my reservations, I went ahead to articulate the programme of action for the ground-breaking ceremony with Chinedu Okpareke. As a mark of his seriousness over the issue, the governor held a follow-up meeting with us some three weeks after the first one. Within a short period after our second meeting, I came up with proposals and estimates which I forwarded to the governor's office. But the expected response did not come. Since I no longer had access to him, I could not ascertain whether he received my proposal or not. Weeks later, I sent a reminder. There was still no response. Looking back now, I can safely say that it is doubtful if those mails actually got to the governor.

Curiously, however, I was to learn later that the governor has constituted a committee for the ground-breaking ceremony of the Imo Wonderlake Resort and Conference Centre. I was neither the chairman nor a member of the committee.

I ended up as an observer. This was in spite of the fact that the major target of the policy thrust of the Ministry of Culture and Tourism as encapsulated in the policy thrusts of the New Face of Imo (the pet policy of the Ohakim administration) was "to develop the Oguta Wonderlake and Abadaba Lake as international tourist attractions."

It was strange that when it was time for implementation, the Commissioner in charge of the relevant ministry was shut out of the plan.

Even though redeployments in government, as I noted earlier, are normal occurrences, mine was trailed by a lot of reactions. Some days or weeks after the incident, I had cause to visit Chief Francis Arthur Nzeribe at his Haven of Peace residence in Oguta. When the man saw me, he said: "Honourable Commissioner, is this your movement a promotion or a demotion?" To this I responded: "Chief, the movement is lateral. It is neither a promotion nor a demotion" He smiled wryly and we rested the matter. But I was introspective enough to imagine what his mind was constructing.

Chief Nzeribe was not alone in such perception of my redeployment. People approached me on the issue in diverse ways. On one particular occasion, the Catechist of the Catholic Church in my community visited my new office. When he was ushered into my office, and after the exchange of pleasantries, I waited for him to say what his mission was. He said that he heard that I had been moved to a new ministry and that he came to confirm what he heard. I did not know whether to read mischief in his action or perceive it as normal. He spoke as if he was on a condolence visit.

Beyond all this, the gossip avenue was awash with comments of different hues. My close associates among the Government House staff came to tell me about those who were celebrating my redeployment among members of the Media Council. They were happy that the man who lorded it over them was no longer favoured in the eyes of the governor.

At my local Government Area level, there were also rumours among my detractors. Those who were feeling that my political ascendancy would constitute a stumbling block to them heaved a sigh of relief. I was told that their concern was not about whichever ministry I was sent to since I remained a Commissioner. Their interest was that the movement has an underlying import. It meant that I was no longer in the good books of the governor and would therefore not have any establishment backing should I step out to contest for public office. The matter appeared to different people in different ways.

But to underline the fact that the redeployment was more impulsive than a calculated measure to reposition the information machinery of the government, the governor did not rejig the Information/Media Council after my exit. I remained the chairman of the council even though there was a new Commissioner for Information and Strategy.

Again, to bring home the fact that the action may not have been well considered, no viable alternative could be found for the ministry after my removal. The ministry ended up with two more Commissioners in the remaining one year. In all, the Ministry of Information and Strategy had four Commissioners in four years under the administration.

Chapter 26

ENTER THE MACHINE GOD

We are told that politics is a game of numbers. We are also told that it is a game of interest. But politics is also a game of circumstance. You could rise or fall in politics based on the sheer force of circumstance. Circumstance can make or mar individuals and institutions both in politics and outside of it. It is like the deus ex machina, the god from a machine in ancient Greek theatre providentially introduced into a situation to solve a difficulty.

Circumstance played a role in the political succession that was witnessed in Imo State in 2011. Before Ohakim's return to PDP in July 2009, some ambitious elements within the party in the State were scheming to use the force and power of the party to neutralize the incumbency of Governor Ikedi Ohakim. They felt that the PDP was stronger than whatever incumbency that the governor may be relying upon.

It all began with Ohakim's plan to return to PDP. We have noted the encouragements which Ohakim got from some respected politicians of Imo extraction, notably, Arthur Nzeribe. We have also underlined the positive remarks on the side of Ohakim from many commentators. But that was just one side to the issue. As Ohakim schemed to return to PDP and take control of the party's machinery in the State, Achike Udenwa, the former governor of the state and, at that time, the Minister of Commerce and Industry who was the leader of the party in the state, was uncomfortable with the unfolding development. Even though he played a prominent role in ensuring the emergence of Ohakim as governor in 2007, both men had fallen apart along the line. The romance between them had ended.

Apart from Udenwa, there was also Ifeanyi Ararume, the PDP candidate in the 2007 governorship elections, who was abandoned by the party in favour of Ohakim, the PPA candidate. Ararume lost grounds on account of circumstance. He won the primary elections of the PDP and was set to emerge as governor when the then president, Olusegun Obasanjo, intervened. Obasanjo did not want Ararume and he ensured that he did not get the blessing of the PDP to win the election.

To realize this objective, the national leadership of the party, by mere fiat, handed over the ticket of the party to Engr. Charles Ugwu who came 5th in the primary elections. Dissatisfied, Ararume sought redress in court. He won. The court asked the PDP to recognize Ararume as its candidate for the April 2007 elections. By the time the court ruled, it was too late for the party's leadership to do anything about the judgement. They allowed Ararume to fly the party's flag. But that was as far as it went. They did not support his candidature. Instead, they adopted the candidate of another party, the PPA, and rallied their support for him. That was how Ohakim emerged as governor in 2007.

Ararume went to court to challenge Ohakim's victory at the polls. He was steadfast in his challenge. But after a long-drawn legal tangle, Ohakim retained his position as governor. Ararume licked his wounds. But, for him, the battle was not over. He waited patiently for 2011 to renew his quest for governorship. He was, before Ohakim began to plan his return, comfortably seated in the PDP. Suddenly, however, the tone of the situation began to change. Ohakim, the incumbent governor, was set to return. If he did, he would automatically become the leader of the party in the State. And if this becomes the case, it would be difficult, if not impossible, for Ararume to have his way in the party. Besides, Ohakim as a first term governor was bound to run for a second term. This scenario presented Ararume with difficulty. He knew that it would not be easy to defeat an incumbent governor in the party's primary. The best bet for him then was to ensure that Ohakim did not return to PDP.

In the face of this set-up, Ararume and Udenwa who, hitherto, were political foes, began to plan how they could join forces to stop Ohakim's return to the PDP. It was in this way that the Destiny Organization and Redemption '98 operated by Ararume and Udenwa respectively, teamed up against Ohakim's New Face Organization. However, despite the opposition by Udenwa and Ararume, Ohakim, through the support of the Yar'Adua presidency and the national leadership of the PDP, succeeded in returning to the party.

But the calculation changed when Ohakim crossed over to PDP. With that development, those who had been waiting in the wings to neutralize his powers through the PDP got stranded. At first they tried to latch on something. They held that Ohakim as a new member of the PDP would not qualify to fly the party's flag in the 2011 governorship elections because he would have spent less than the number of months stipulated by the party's constitution to qualify as candidate. But that road block did not work. Ohakim circumvented it. The governor was cruising home to be the unchallenged king of Imo politics of the time. The governor's hold on power became even more assured with the Yar'Adua presidency. The president and the governor had a closeness that detractors could not destroy. When therefore Yar'Adua took ill, Ohakim was one of the close confidantes of the president that did not jump ship. He remained steadfast. He stood by the president until death snatched him away.

With the death of Yar'Adua, a new circumstance stepped in to alter the political calculation in the country. The politics of Imo was affected by this circumstance. The ascension of Goodluck Jonathan as president presented the country with a new scenario. In Imo State, Ohakim's detractors who had lost hold of the PDP sprang up again. They started a fresh campaign of calumny against him. They told the new president (Jonathan) that Ohakim was a member of the clique of Yar'Adua loyalists who were opposed to the introduction of the Doctrine of Necessity that made him the acting president. The impression they sold to Jonathan was that Ohakim played the role they accused him of because he wanted to take over Jonathan's job as vice president by 2011.

As the head of Ohakim's media team at the time, I joined issues with the governor's detractors. My goal then was to clarify the situation and get the president to understand and appreciate the issue as it really was.

While the campaign for and against Ohakim lasted, Jonathan, ever reticent and calm, did not betray any emotions. It was therefore difficult to know what he believed or did not believe. But then, Ohakim himself did not leave the matter lying low. He worked hard enough to penetrate Jonathan, culminating in the State visit of Mr. President to Imo State. The president was lavishly received by the people and government of Imo State. He was finally crowned and decorated as "Chinemeze" by the then Chairman of Imo State Council of Traditional Rulers, Eze Cletus Ikechukwu Ilomuanya, at a colourful ceremony. With the visit over, Ohakim was rest assured that Jonathan was properly disposed to him. With this impression, Ohakim did not have to operate like an orphan governor who did not have the backing and protection of a godfather. Rather, he operated like a serving governor of the ruling party at both the State and Federal levels which he was. This set-up guaranteed him a reasonable level of comfort and protection.

But this was one end of the stick on the issue. The other end was held by those who were ill at ease with the new rapprochement that existed between Jonathan and Ohakim. This state of affairs led to the defection of Ararume and Udenwa to the rival Action Congress of Nigeria (ACN). While Ararume picked up the ticket of the party as its governorship candidate, Udenwa stepped out to run for the Senate seat in his senatorial zone. By this time, Ohakim had also emerged as the governorship candidate of the PDP. The battle line was therefore drawn. It was between Ohakim, the PDP candidate, and the breakaway faction of the party which had moved over to ACN.

At this stage, the All Progressives Grand Alliance (APGA) was not a factor. Rochas Okorocha had also not yet emerged as its candidate. In fact, Rochas was a late comer to the governorship scene in 2011. He declared his ambition when virtually all the other parties had known who their candidates would be. However, with Okorocha's emergence as the candidate of APGA, the circumstance of the Imo 2011 gubernatorial election assumed a new dimension. Ohakim was firmly in control of the State apparatus of the PDP, but he did not imagine that it could be possible that the president may not be very properly disposed to his return as second term governor. However, certain signs of duplicity on the part of the authorities in Abuja began to emerge in the thick of the campaigns. While the presidency recognized and accepted Ohakim as the PDP candidate for the elections, it was also hobnobbing with the candidate of a rival political party- Rochas Okorocha of APGA. The romance between Rochas and the Presidency was so open that Rochas displayed in front of his campaign headquarters in Owerri his photograph and that of the president framed together. With that romantic liaison between Jonathan and Okorocha as epitomized by the framed photograph, it was no longer clear where the president belonged.

For many people, that pictorial display by Rochas was dismissed as part of his campaign gimmick. But discerning minds within the Imo PDP received it with mixed feelings. Even though this was the case, there was no visible cause for worry. After all, Ohakim was the incumbent and all those who claim to know everything about Nigerian politics had said that it was not possible to dislodge him in his quest for a second term in office. In fact, the permutations of the Nzeribes of this world who had, for decades, bestridden Nigerian politics like a colossus gave the PDP and its candidate all the confidence they needed. If Nzeribe, a supposed master of the game had spoken, who could speculate otherwise.

It was on the strength of this misplaced confidence that the elections began. But if the issue was a matter of speculation before the elections, its import manifested clearly when the elections began. The National Assembly elections came first. It was very peaceful in Imo State. Military personnel were not deployed to monitor the elections. PDP, the ruling party in the state, won majority of the seats. This was followed by the presidential elections. The atmosphere during that election was much more relaxed. There was no harassment or intimidation of any sort. And there were no military personnel anywhere in the streets. Jonathan, the PDP candidate, also won very decisively.

Strangely, all of that changed on the day of the Governorship and House of Assembly elections. Suddenly, Imo became militarized. Military personnel armed to the teeth were deployed everywhere in the state, particularly the voting areas. The PDP, the ruling party in the country and in the state, which won the first two elections overwhelmingly, became suddenly disadvantaged. The party's stalwarts and agents in the State were treated in many places on that day as if they had been marked out for harassment and intimidation. Imo was on edge. People lost their basic freedoms while the election lasted.

As all this was going on, we, members of the Ohakim team, monitored the situation across the state from our various wards. We made frantic telephone calls to know what was going on in various local government areas. The reports we got showed that Okorocha, contrary to our expectation, was making appreciable impact in many areas. But that was not enough to upset the apple carte. Elections were held in all the 27 Local Government Areas of the State except Ngor Okpala. From the figures before us, Ohakim would have won the elections had all the results from the 26 Local government areas where elections held been declared.

Then as if to lend credence to the suspicion that the presidency was not bothered whether the PDP won the state or not, it looked the other way while the Independent National Electoral Commission (INEC) did the unimaginable. It cancelled the results of Ohaji/Egbema and Oguta Local government Areas, the two local government Areas that formed part of Ohakim's mainstay. Ohakim, as expected, won convincingly in the two councils. Thus, of the 24 council areas whose results were declared, Ohakim scored 25 percent of the votes cast in 18 while Rochas won in 17. However, the total number of votes scored by Rochas was slightly higher than Ohakim's. But Rochas could not be declared winner because he failed to secure the 25 percent spread in two thirds of the local government areas of the state. With this set-up, the election was declared inconclusive by INEC. A supplementary election was to be held in order for a winner to emerge.

Chapter 27

REALITY SETS IN

For Governor Ohakim and his team, what transpired on that election day was like a story from a book. It looked unreal. It was as if someone just woke up from a trance. The conspiracy theory which people conjured up silently began to make meaning. The concerned relapsed into introspective analysis. Why was Imo under military siege on that day? Who ordered the deployment of soldiers and to what end? There were many nagging questions begging for answers.

When you leave the deployment of soldiers out of it, you then begin to worry about the cancellation of the results of the elections in Ohaji/Egbema and Oguta, two local government areas where Ohakim won with a wide margin. In this, observers began to smell conspiracy. The impression it created was that the authorities in Abuja set out to undermine Ohakim and put him in a disadvantaged position. Then, you began to wonder why a serving governor from the ruling party at the federal and state levels should be subjected to this state of disadvantage by agents and agencies of the federal government. What went wrong? Who was behind the plot? Those were some of the questions that poured out in torrents from curious minds.

But because the time was too short to resolve these issues, the supplementary elections did not change anything. In Oguta local government area, a group of hoodlums held everybody to ransom. They said that they did not want elections in Oguta LGA because they suspected that forces loyal to Ohakim would manipulate the process to his advantage. The military which had been deployed to ensure that the elections went smoothly could not stop them. They stood by and watched the brigandage with sardonic satisfaction. The police personnel did not act differently. They seemed to be part of the agenda to ensure that Oguta was blacked out. At the end of the day, no election held in Oguta. This development put Ohakim at a great disadvantage. An incumbent governor, contrary to what analysts and bookmakers said, had been castrated. His incumbency had been rendered impotent. An outsider who no one thought could pose a threat to the incumbent had become the beautiful bride. The powers and the forces seemed to have embraced him and his party, leaving desolate the ruling party and its incumbent governor. That was how Ohakim was denied the mandate to govern Imo for a second term. The development, strange as it was, remains one of the wonders and puzzles of Nigeria's politics of the Fourth Republic.

Even after Ohakim's loss, more questions continued to tumble in. What went wrong or what could have been wrong? How come that the permutations, assumptions and predictions of the oracles of politics did not come to pass? How come that their conclusions which, in political circles, were taken as articles of faith, went off the mark? Why was incumbency stripped of its fangs without a whimper? The Imo, and indeed, the Nigerian political landscape, were awash with these puzzling questions at that point in time.

In trying to pigeonhole the situation, many attributed the great fall to the personality of Ohakim. The received impression in many quarters at the time was that Ohakim was consumed by the allure of power; that hubris - that scornful, overweening pride which ultimately leads to a tragic fall, took the better part of him. Ohakim, at that time, was perceived in many quarters as an arrogant governor who was unmindful of the mood of the people that elected him. Many complained that his public speeches, particularly those rendered extempore, were an unmitigated display of haughtiness and disdain for the people. Those of us who were part of the government were regularly confronted with these charges. But we explained them away as they came.

As the elections drew closer, many people who were close to me had cause to join issues with me concerning the governor. They told me that my boss was going to lose the election. I told them that it was not possible. As someone who once had the responsibility of propagating and explaining the activities and actions of government, I usually took on my interlocutors on the successes of the Ohakim administration which qualified him for re-election. But again, as one of them always said: "But the people do not see these things the way you have presented them." In fact, arguments bordering on the governor were on every minute in every corner of Imo state at that time.

The culmination of all this for me was an anonymous text message I got about a month to the election. Someone had sent this to my mobile phone with a number that was not registered in it. It read: "Your boss, Ikedi Ohakim will not return as the governor of Imo State. Therefore begin to restrategise." When I read this, I decided to call the number. But the fellow bounced off the call. Before I could come to terms with his action, he fired again with another text message. He said: "You don't need to know me. Just take what I have told you." After reading this, I gazed vacantly into space, not knowing what to think or say.

It was under this atmosphere of resentment for Ohakim on account of his approach to public issues that Rochas Okorocha stepped in. Whereas most governorship aspirants were known early enough by the people, Okorocha was the last to join the race.

As a street-wise politician, he gauged the mood of the people. He was aware that an atmosphere of resentment pervaded the Imo landscape. There may not have been any good ground for the level of resentment that was visited on the governor. But it caught on like a contagion. Okorocha cashed in on this state of affairs. He began to appeal to the emotions and sentiments of the ordinary people of Imo State. Whereas Ohakim was packaged and sold as being insensitive to their feelings, Okorocha began to ride and attitudinize with the keke (tricycle) riders. He began to embrace market women in the streets and ate from the same plate with them. He sang everyday songs that gave the impression that he was a home-bred, public-spirited fellow who understood the people and felt their pain. Consequently, they began to embrace him. They began to be fanatical about him. All this may have made a lot of difference in the eyes of the people. But those of us who were on the side of government saw things differently.

Chapter 28

PHOTO FINISH

In fact, all the signs were there that the electoral contest between Ohakim and Okorocha was going to be tough. But it was hardly clear to anybody, including those who were passionate about Okorocha. Not even the incident on the day of the Governorship Debate organized by the Catholic Archdiocese of Owerri could have a sobering influence on us. On that day, governorship candidates of the different political parties had converged on Obiri Odenigbo area of the Villa Assumpta, the Owerri Archdiocesan headquarters of the Catholic Church. Ohakim came in when most of them were already seated and went round to have a handshake with them, one after the other. When he got to where Okorocha was seated, he (Okorocha) stood up and they embraced each other rapturously. Then they disengaged and went for a handshake. But this turned into a contest. Their right hands were locked together. They held them aloft to the excitement of the audience. Each tried to outdo the other in this exercise. One wanted his hand to be on top. The other would not allow that. As they struggled in this friendly encounter, the audience went wild with excitement. It was a photo finish. The mock contest lasted for sometime before they lowered their hands. Looking back, it could be said that the close race that the election turned out to be actually manifested on that fateful day at Villa Assumpta. But we could not, owing to our limited understanding as human beings, interpret the situation appropriately at that point in time.

Even when the debate began, it was only the governor and Okorocha that caught the attention of the people. Ohakim had begun his address with a preamble which bordered on the hardship in the land. Knowing the way the governor speaks, I knew that he was going to navigate his address into the mainstream of the issue of the day. Unfortunately, an unruly crowd cashed in on the reference he was making to the hardship in the land and the suffering of the people. Their unspoken conclusion was that a sitting governor who had admitted that the people were suffering had nothing more to tell the people. They went wild with shouts of disapproval. They did not want the governor to continue. The atmosphere became almost riotous. The governor had touched raw nerves. And the people shouted freely at him. His Grace, Most Reverend Anthony JV Obinna, the Catholic Archbishop of OwerrI, had to intervene severally before calm returned. Ohakim resumed his speech. But he had already been destabilized by the crowd. He had to round off quickly to avoid incurring the people's wrath a second time.

Then came Okorocha. There was hardly any substance to his speech. He basically appealed to the emotions and sentiments of the people. His speech was full of abstractions. He even employed vocabularies that do not exist in the English Language. Yet, such semi-literate usages excited the people. They held him in high esteem. There was excitement in the air. That was the mood that pervaded the atmosphere on that day. The main contenders had spoken and people were beginning to leave the venue in trickles. While I was stepping out of the place, I met a white garment pastor from my community who was also on his way out. We exchanged pleasantries and then he said: "The next governor has spoken", referring to Okorocha.

When the election was eventually held and Okorocha was declared winner, the anonymous messenger returned to me. This time he said: "I told you that Ohakim would not return as governor." Like before, I called the number but he refused to pick. When I shared this experience with a few friends, one of them told me that the message from that fellow was a spiritual revelation which he said I could not, as an ordinary mortal, fathom at that point in time. Since I was not given to superstition, I dismissed his interjection with a wave of the hand. And we went on to discuss other issues.

Chapter 29

POLITICS NIGERIANA

Nigeria, in nearly six decades of its independence, has had a chequered political history. Like most things Nigerian, there has been a progressive decline in the quality of Nigerian politics. The country's First Republic had its own brand of politics. Then, the principal players were the educated elite and other patriots who had a running battle with the colonialists in order to free the country from their over lordship. Having succeeded in dislodging the foreigners from political control of the country, the Nigerian elite took over the reins of governance. Unfortunately, they could not consolidate the gains of independence. The political actors were soon to be torn apart by divisive tendencies. Politics assumed a regional or sectional garb and the country was, willy nilly, divided along these lines.

Having been left to run their own affairs, Nigerians were to discover that their oneness was a tenuous one. Politicians began to appeal freely and recklessly to ethnic sentiments. People who came together to fight against foreign rule suddenly realized that their claim to being Nigerians was limited and constrained by primordial considerations. The divisive tendencies boiled over when the country held its first general elections in 1964. It was largely flawed. Boycott, murder and arson were its defining characteristics. In trying to manage the patchwork that the colonialists had bequeathed to them, the battle for supremacy and domination among the major ethnic nationalities was soon to graduate into ethnic hate. Rather than fashion out a road map that would give the country an enduring brand of politics, the politicians got embroiled in battles for ethnic advantage. The set-up, in no time, got out of hand and the military, which had been waiting in the wings, intervened. Civil rule ended and the military took over the reins of governance.

After 13 long years of military interregnum part of which was spent in prosecuting a fratricidal civil war, the military grudgingly returned the country to civil rule.

The politics of the Second Republic which began in 1979 had its own defining characteristics. The quality of the practitioners had dropped. The intervention of the military had not only plundered the system, it had unleashed on the country a crop of ill-educated, semi-literate officers and men who reduced governance to the reign of force and brigandage. The intellectual and robust engagements which the Nnamdi Azikiwes, the Obafemi Awolowos, the Ahmadu Bellos, the Mbonu Ojikes and other fire brand politicians brought to the political scene had given way to the brashness and incivility of the ruling military junta. This bastardization of the system had a telling effect on the politics of the Second Republic. Apart from the decline in the quality of the practitioners, those who strutted into the scene demonstrated through their actions that they had learnt nothing from the country's nasty political experience. This being the case, brazenness became the order of the day. Again, the military watched with sardonic pleasure, ready to strike. They waited eagerly for an opportunity to play the martial music. Then came the 1983 elections which the political players conducted. The exercise was messed up. The elections were brazenly rigged. It was an opportunity the military had been waiting for. They struck again and the country relapsed into the reign of the jackboot. But the military intervention of 31st December, 1983, led by Major

General Muhammadu Buhari did not endure. There was distrust and infighting within the military high command. In no time, the new government ran into a storm. The result was the overthrow of the Buhari regime by General Ibrahim Babangida in August, 1985.

But the story, this time, was not quite rosy for the military. Their many years of intrusion into governance had not improved the lot of the country. The aberration that is military incursion into politics had become very manifest. The citizenry were therefore ill at ease with military rule. However, to stave off civil agitations for a return to democratic governance, the new military junta led by Babangida began to toy with the idea of returning power to civilians within the shortest possible time. The first date Babangida set for the exercise was 1990. But within the intervening period, he set up a Politburo with which he kept the country busy and diverted their attention from the real issues of the time. The Politburo was modeled after its equivalent in the former Soviet Union as a principal policy-making committee. Its assignment was to engage Nigerians on what they considered the best form of political system that would serve the peculiar needs and circumstances of the country. The offer from government looked attractive and Nigerians spent valuable time brainstorming on it. By the time the Politburo concluded its assignment, Babangida had gathered enough moss. He had found good reason to move the terminal date of his administration from 1990 to 1993. With this new date in place, the government established two political parties, the Social Democratic Party (SDP), and the National Republican Convention (NRC). Then the jostle for political offices began in earnest. To give a semblance of seriousness to his political agenda, elections to fill political offices in the states were held in 1991, two clear years to the planned handover date to civilians. Thus, while we had a military president at the centre, there were civilian governors in the states. National and State Assembly elections were also held to complement the arrangement. The new order gave rise to diarchy, a political arrangement in which the military and civilians shared political power. This idea was consistently advocated by Nnamdi Azikiwe in those heady days of military rule as a way of finding some space for civilians in governance. Babangida eventually adopted it not by design but by default.

With the partial involvement of civilians in governance, feverish preparations began for the 1993 presidential elections. The government of the day came up with what it called "New Breed Politicians". They were the ones government could trust. It banned as many "Old Breed Politicians" as it wanted from participating in politics. It was the idea of new breed politicians that threw up an MKO Abiola. He had not played politics before; therefore, government had no reason to ban him from taking part in the political process. Abiola came into politics with unusual energy. He broke into political and institutional strongholds. In no time, he permeated circles that were, hitherto, thought to be impregnable. The military which midwifed the June 12, 1993 presidential elections, was evidently ill prepared for the Abiola onslaught. When the election eventually held, he made remarkable in roads and was set to win. But that was not what the military wanted. They did not know that the Abiola aspiration would be real. They would not let that be. Consequently, the election was annulled. The development put the country on edge and a crisis of immense proportion began.

Given the tension in the land, Babangida could not consider the option of staying in office beyond 1993. He had to find a way out. This eventuated in the enthronement of a hurriedly concocted Interim National Government led by Chief Earnest Shonekan. But because the arrangement was ill-conceived and ill-thought out, it could not handle the intricate issues of statecraft. The government was like a wingless bee; a lame duck structure that could not hold its own. General Sani Abacha, another military adventurer, saw through the lacuna. It was a beautiful opportunity for him to step in. And he did. Thus, in less than four months after the enthronement of the Interim National Government, it was dismantled by Abacha. On ascension to power, Abacha dismantled all the democratic structures put in place by Babangida. The country returned once again to full scale military rule.

But Abiola would take none of that. He wanted the government to release the result of the June 12, 1993 elections in which he was leading the candidate of the NRC, Bashir Othman Tofa, before it was annulled. Frustrated that his presumed victory was being discountenanced, Abiola, with the encouragement of pro-democracy campaigners, particularly the National Democratic Coalition (NADECO), made the famous Epetedo declaration at which he declared himself president. The Abacha government saw the declaration as an affront. In fact, it considered it treasonable. It was tantamount to having two sovereigns within a sovereign state. For this reason, Abiola was arrested and clamped into detention. With his arrest and detention, the agitation for the revalidation of the results of the June 12, 1993 elections assumed a feverish dimension. There was an outcry by the civil populace. Pro-democracy and human rights activists seized the stage. They confronted the Abacha regime with all the arsenal at their disposal. Then Abacha had to fight back. The Nigerian environment became charged. The Abacha government went after the agitators. Many of them were hounded into exile. There were also cases of assassination as the government intensified its effort to rein in the protesters.

Perhaps as a ploy to divert some attention from the agitators, the Abacha government set up a National Constitutional Conference. The conference was aimed at bringing Nigerians together to discuss the future of their country. The conference was to provide the constitutional and institutional framework for a better administration and governance of the country. The forum provided Nigerians with a fertile ground. This occupied their attention between 1994 and 1995.

Unlike Babangida before him who Nigerians accused of plotting openly to elongate his stay in office owing to his style, Abacha adopted a radically different approach in his bid to elongate his stay in office. Abacha was largely reticent. Yet his silences were loud. He was even given away the more by an army of agitators who entertained Nigerians with histrionics. There was, for instance, the Daniel Kanu-led "Youths Earnestly Ask for Abacha." The group organized a two million-man march requesting Abacha to transmute to a civilian president, but Abacha did not respond to their request. Such agitations became almost a daily fare. They became widespread. Then it was the turn of the five political parties that came into existence under Abacha's reign. Rather than choose presidential candidates who would stand for elections, the five parties unanimously adopted Abacha as their consensus candidate. They asked him to transmute to a civilian president. Yet, Abacha kept mum. But in spite of his studied silence, it was clear that everything was programmed to have him as Nigeria's civilian president. The pro-Abacha plot proceeded side by side with the agitations of those who wanted Abiola to be released and sworn in as the president of the country. The crisis lasted for five years without respite. Then some conspirators took over. They presided over the elimination of Abacha from the scene and that effectively marked the end of the Abacha plot. But if they thought that the death of Abacha would bring respite to the country, it did not. Rather, it emboldened the June 12 agitators the more. They began to demand vociferously for the release of Abiola. They also wanted him to be sworn in as the president of Nigeria on his release. With this, it was clear to the plotters that they still had work to do. Thus, within one month of Abacha's death, Abiola also died in mysterious circumstances. That effectively ended the five-year old political crisis that engulfed the country.

This state of affairs fouled the political atmosphere in Nigeria. It left many with the impression that Nigeria was still in the Hobbesian state of nature where life was nasty, brutish and short. The set-up brought to life the mechanistic doctrine of the end justifies the means which Nicolo Machiavelli, the Italian Renaissance political philosopher and statesman, was known for. These upheavals took place in Nigeria and yet the masterminds and executors remained on the scene and continued to determine the direction of the country's politics. The rest of the people queued behind them either sheepishly or helplessly.

Then to demonstrate to the people that they are the executors and executioners of their dreams, the powerful hands, both seen and unseen, plotted the way forward. They put in place a new political transition that would produce one of their own - a retired army general as the next president. This was the grand design. The rest of the political flock fell over one another as much as they could. They thought they would have a role to play in enthroning the next president of Nigeria. But they were utterly mistaken. Those who know the under belly of Nigeria had done the job for the rest of the people. These determinants of the political future of the country and the fortune or misfortune of the players were to become the focal points of Nigeria's politics. They became what in the country's politics is now loosely referred to as "godfathers". Then the anointed ones, with the backing of the all-powerful godfathers, became the brand new headache the polity had to face. Owing to the manner of their ascendancy, arrogance of power crept in. They owe their allegiance not to the people but to the privileged class that enthroned them. All this brought about brigandage and effrontery into Nigerian politics.

I have undertaken this historical excursion so as to put in proper perspective how Nigeria's politics got bastardized. When we talk of lowering of standards and the desecration of the political space in the land, we cannot but remind ourselves of this wolfish trajectory that the country has passed through. With this experience and culture of impunity, Nigerian politics has acquired all the ugly attributes that lead to self-destruction. The salutary side of politics has been thrown overboard, leaving the people with a bastardized set-up. To keep pace with the ugly trend, Nigerian politics now proceeds with frenetic speed. The struggle for political space approximates to a Trojan horse invasion. Its ruthlessness is unsparing. It has no pity or sympathy for those who cannot cope with its speed and ravages. All this is happening because the years of plunder by the military have disoriented the people. The people's political psyche now dreams corruption and primitive acquisition. The people's brains have been polluted and their imagination corrupted.

This situation has, to a very large extent, alienated the educated elite and the socially refined. This class of Nigerians has been thoroughly scandalized by the practice in the land. They have been unable to come to terms with the brigandage and pillaging that have been going on. Consequently, a good many of them have withdrawn into their shells. But this has even a more telling effect on the political environment. The mediocrities and jackals which the bastardized system has thrown up have seized the stage. They have reduced politics to their own level. They have divested the system of whatever decency it has. If politics in Nigeria qualifies as a dirty game, we can trace this unenviable tag to the miscreants that rule and reign in the polity.

In Nigeria, when a tutored mind ventures into the murky waters of Nigerian politics, he is bound to feel claustrophobic at first before getting used to the foggy atmosphere. In most cases, most intellectuals do not get accustomed to the treachery and bad blood that define the game of politics. If you must thrive in the political arena, you are, in most cases, expected to bring yourself to the level of howlers who see politics as an ultimate enterprise. Owing to this ruthless nature of Nigerian politics, many of the practitioners get caught in the frenzy. This is especially so of people who lose their head to the dictates of the game. Even those who manage to retain their sanity, more often than not, tend to lose it during electioneering campaigns.

Chapter 30

MY POLITICAL BAPTISM

As the government we served in Imo state between 2007 and 2011 moved closer to elections, I came face to face with Nigerian politics at its most banal. One particular Monday morning, I stood with two or three of my colleagues in front of the Executive Council Chambers within Government House. As we were waiting for the Executive Council meeting to begin, we decided to reflect on the situation around us. After taking a hard look at the political atmosphere and how it was affecting governance, I remarked thus: "Politics is a very difficult way of earning a living".

This remark caught the attention and fancy of one of my colleagues – George Irechukwu – who was the Commissioner for Finance. George agreed with me completely. He probably was thinking along the same line as myself. As part of the government, I had experienced spite. I had been brow-beaten. Sometimes a certain air of despondency would envelop the environment. I squirmed at this state of siege. The discomfort was telling. I pitied myself and every other person who felt the way I felt. George as the controller of government finance may not have felt exactly the way I felt. But he understood what I meant.

If you were reasonably comfortable where you were before government pulled you away and put you on the path of wilful impoverishment, you are bound to look back in time with a view to comparing between the past and the present. If you were gainfully employed or meaningfully engaged and felt you were not an object of public scrutiny, chances are that you will have a reasonable level of peace of mind. But when government makes you the cynosure without commensurate remuneration to deal with the situation, things would definitely be different for you as you are likely to face derision in the eyes of those who consider public office as a bounty or booty.

The election year of 2011 when the government we served was seeking re-election brought all this into bold relief. As the elections approached, we, government officials, were told to spend less time in our offices. We were told to relocate to our local government areas and wards and get close to the electorate. That was the best way to ensure the victory of your party at the polls. They told us that in politics, you cannot afford to lose election in your ward. That such loss could spell doom for your political career. The assumption here is that once you are appointed to serve, you must necessarily play politics. That is why political office holders are automatically registered as members of the ruling party. You do not have a choice here. And so we joined the political campaign train from the ward to the state level. I must confess that the confusion of that period was troubling. Those months were harrowing. I was brought face to face with upstarts in the name of politics. I was made to relate with people with little or no education whose world view or approach to issues was diametrically opposed to mine.

In the same political arena, you literally did battle with benighted souls who have neither brain nor imagination. You were almost lost in a sea of howlers. Inconsequential backwood people were all over the place. Some even had the temerity to trade tackles with men of learning and intellect. They see the political field as a leveller. You are at everybody's level in so far as you are a part of the game. I found all this confusing, even agonizing. I looked at a good number of the people involved with disdain. I merely tolerated them. But no matter how much discomfort you feel, you must remain on the campaign train. You have to be part of the madding crowd. Yes, the season was one of madness. The office was partially on holiday. Your brief has suddenly changed. You are now in the eye of the storm. You are caught in the political chase game. It did not matter what your preferences or idiosyncrasies dictated.

My agony was prolonged by the fact that the governorship election of that year was scheduled three times. On the original day the election was to hold nationwide, it was postponed by the Independent National Electoral Commission for some reason. The postponement made nonsense of all our earlier preparations. In politics, patronage has a very short life span. The people you gratify this week for whatever political gain will expect you to do the same thing for them the following week if you still require their patronage. Indeed, patronage has no second hand value in Nigerian politics. For this reason, whatever investment we made on the people expired with the postponement of the election. We had to repeat the ritual for the rescheduled election. Again, and unfortunately for all of us on the side of government, the outcome of the election, when it eventually held, was not quite favourable. But for me particularly, the agony was more telling because the result of the election in my local government area was not upheld by the electoral commission. A supplementary election was scheduled for May 6, 2011 in four local government areas of the state, including mine. But again, the situation in my council area proved intractable. Hoodlums and hired thugs ensured that the election did not hold in my local government area. The result was eventually declared without the input from my council area.

When eventually the whole episode came to an end on May 29, 2011, a new year began for me. What was of significance to me was that I reprogrammed my brain after the election was won and lost. Looking back, I am convinced that the political appointment served its purpose.

The point must be made that my decision to serve my State was not reached in a hurry. It was well-considered. That was why I approached my assignment with utmost zeal and dedication. I had, before then, been in the business of media consultancy at very high levels. Indeed, I was easily recognized by those who had cause to require my services as an aggressive publicist. I therefore had no difficulty in adjusting to the demands of public service, especially in the area of media relations and information management. However, in every new assignment one undertakes, there is always a time to play the virgin. There is always the age and time of innocence. Usually, the practitioner is at his idealistic best when his mind or imagination has not been corrupted by the environment. Such a corruption of the mind, when it happens, can lead to withdrawal or disillusionment. It is one disease which afflicts many, including those who set out to give their environment their best. If the affliction strikes without warning, it usually stifles vision and vitiates the vibrancy and vitality that should drive change and performance. That is why many tend to go livid on arrival when they should be soaring to high heavens with their creative imagination.

But as a developed mind who places much premium on the imagination, I usually relapse into the realm of ratiocination to deal with such developments. That way, I strive to demolish those structures that seek to put me down. That is why it is difficult to catch me napping. Indeed, I was under no illusion when I chose to step into the arena of public service. I almost saw through the end from the very beginning.

With that, I decided that one thing that must guide my actions and inactions, thenceforth, is the experience I acquired. Experience, largely speaking, has a sobering influence on people. With it, you know why certain things are what they are. Experience puts you in a position to appreciate your environment more dispassionately. But it manifests in diverse ways and forms in people. For some, it leads to a certain life of moroseness and resignation. For others, it challenges the imagination to begin to seek alternatives to systems and attitudes that have not helped the cause of humanity. Beyond that, experience takes you back in time. It reminds you of where you were coming from and jolts you into realizing where you have eventually found yourself.

Most new entrants into politics, especially those who are coming from very sane professions, usually suffer a culture shock the moment they confront the political environment. A renowned professional who has been called to serve will usually approach his job, at the very beginning, with zeal and verve. He can offer anything to ensure that he lives up to expectation. But that is the ideal. The real situation is that while he strives to make a remarkable difference in his area of operation, detractors and mischief-makers will be laying land mines for him. They want him to stumble. They do not want good stories told about him. They are afraid that positive remarks will take him to a higher height. He must therefore not be allowed to excel. He must be kept at the level of the howlers.

I recall that my boss at The Guardian Newspapers, Mr. Kingsley Osadolor, warned me against the land mines when he called to congratulate me on my appointment as Commissioner for Information and Strategy. Osadolor himself had then just returned from Edo State where he served as Commissioner. He was talking from experience. But the uninitiated would hardly understand, let alone appreciate, such remarks. I heard him quite all right but I was to learn much later in the course of my assignment in Owerri that I did not quite appreciate the wisdom in his advice when it was offered.

Politics in these shores also reminds you of the anti-intellectual culture which rules our public sphere. The lot of the intellectual in Nigerian politics is not enviable. You may be admired by a few, but an army of others loathes you secretly and silently. They will associate you, almost compulsively, with a certain air of arrogance. Consequently, men and women of intellect can easily find themselves in political wilderness if they do not tone down on their ideals. Unfortunately, to seek to do this is, in itself, an act of self-destruction. It usually yields a counter-productive result. You cannot impress a breed that operates below your mental level by pretending to be like them. But what compounds our problem in this land is that it is such a breed of rascals that are identified and called politicians in Nigeria. Many of them are even proud to tell you that they are politicians as if there is a badge of honour that goes with the name. Then, you begin to wonder whether there is anything edifying about being called a politician.

Unfortunately, no matter the level of disdain you have for this crude breed, the system must bring you face to face with them. You must meet them in the political field. Our system is such that government alone does not suffice. You may be an expert in your area of concentration and may be making the best of impact in that regard, but there is always time to keep all that aside and face politics. In other words, government and politics, even for the man who has been called to serve, must meet, but one does not depend on the other. They stand independently. Your performance in one does not rub off on the other. You may succeed in one and fail in the other. That is the unholy mix between government and politics. Significantly too, this mix has no formula. It depends on what the moment brings. It also differs from one locality to another. But the debilitating thing about all of this is that it slows down our march towards progress. It also cripples vision and the creative instinct in the individual who originally set out to make a difference.

Chapter 31

PRACTICAL POLITICS

The return of civil rule in Nigeria was not just a watershed in the political history of the country, it also marked a significant turning point for a number of non state actors who, nonetheless, were deeply immersed in the politics of the country in some other ways. I was one such person. By May 1999 when Nigeria shed the yoke of military incursion into politics, I was already an enthusiastic analyst who broached virtually every major issue in national discourse. My interventions were well weaned. They came from the heart. They were the genuine concerns of a patriot who felt that his country could be better governed.

As an editor and columnist, I beamed constant searchlight on political actors. My commentaries were deep and compelled attention. It was in this way that a good number of the political players at the time came to recognise me as a strong voice of reason. My interface with governmental power began in this way. It is worthy of note that my interactions with most of the political actors that I encountered during the first leg of the Fourth Republic revealed one thing. A good many of them did not appear prepared for the assignment they had undertaken. They looked more like people who took a chance to fill some vacuums that existed at that time. The unpreparedness of some of the elected persons at that time, including governors, became very clear to me when I undertook a tour of many states of the federation to interview the newly elected governors. LEADERS & Co., the magazine on the stable of THISDAY which I edited, had set out for an ambitious scheme. We wanted to report the governors in a way that no other publication was able to do at that time. That was what got me to set sail. My encounters with the political players was quite revealing and were fully amplified on the pages of the editions of the magazine published at that time.

The sheer incompetence and unpreparedness of many of the political office holders at that time was of concern to those of us who felt and still feel that Nigeria should and could be better governed. I personally felt that the gaps noticed in many of them should be filled by better qualified people. This feeling of disappointment in the quality of most of our representatives at various levels was the major factor that fired my ambition to go to the National Assembly. I wanted to make a clear difference.

It is also significant to note that the tricky transition programmes which Nigeria witnessed from Babangida to Abacha did not help the politics of the immediate post military rule era. Many were skeptical about the sincerity of the military to return power to civilians. Based on this feeling of suspicion, some of those who would have wished to step out for political office fought shy. They stayed away.

However, four years after the experiment began, some confidence had been built on the new political order and more actors had stepped forward to be part of the system. But it did not significantly change the quality of those elected at various levels. After the 2003 elections, I firmed up my resolve to join the political fray. To give effect to my seriousness, I, in 2006, registered as a member of the Peoples Democratic Party Having done that, I began consultations and consequently declared interest to run for the House of Representatives seat in my federal constituency.

In Nigerian politics, godfathers exist and they are not easy to ignore especially for new entrants into the political arena. In my political catchment area, Senator Arthur Nzeribe loomed large at that time. It was considered unwise for a budding politician not to pay homage to Nzeribe. I did and intimated him of my ambition. He welcomed the idea but asked me how much I had for the election. I told him. He told me that that was not enough. He then invited me over to his Haven of Peace residence in Oguta so that we could discuss the matter in detail. I accepted his invitation and promised to visit him within weeks. I returned to Lagos days later. I never kept the appointment with Nzeribe. I did not call him to explain why, and I did not run for the 2007 election.

My handicap then was my job. On my return to Lagos then, I reflected further on my plan to venture into elective politics. I weighed the option of quitting my job as a much sought after senior journalist and venturing into an election that I was not sure of winning. The conclusion I reached after due consideration was that it was an expensive gamble. I therefore decided to keep my political ambition in abeyance. I decided that I would spend more time on the job before venturing into politics.

When I later visited Nzeribe after the 2007 elections, I wanted to explain my constraint. But the man already understood. Without waiting for me to explain, he simply remarked: "You were still enjoying your job". He was right. I was still enjoying my job. I continued to enjoy my job until I was eventually pulled out in February 2009 by Governor Ikedi Ohakim to serve as Honourable Commissioner. The appointment immersed me into practical politics. I did not have any choice any more. That was how my political journey began.

THE INFLUENCERS

Even though I was firmly resolved to take a shot at elective politics as part of the effort to rescue Nigerian politics from lowness and mediocrity, my resolve was boosted the more by some political actors whom I felt were using their privileged political positions to lift the country out of the pit of darkness. Besides, as someone who had been riding the crest through public affairs analyses, I needed some reality tests that would help me to descend from my olympian heights. Fortunately, I was able to learn some useful lessons from some political players whose actions and activities in politics deviated from the ugly and anaemic trend that we are used to. One such person was Peter Obi who was serving as the governor of Anambra State at the time I was trying my hands on elective politics.

Obi's entry into politics was heralded by an uncommon incident. He ran election to the office of the governor of Anambra state in 2003. He won. But his victory was stolen by some political marauders. In Nigerian politics, it is not unusual to upturn people's victories. Such developments are usually played down and accepted by most of those involved. It was therefore almost axiomatic before Peter Obi happened upon the scene that election victories could be procured. But Obi rose against the buccaneers and power mongers at very great odds. His decision to challenge the outcome of the election which he ran under the banner of All Progressives Grand Alliance (APGA) was borne out of conviction. The Electoral Commission had returned Dr Chris Ngige of the PDP as the winner of that election. He was, consequently, sworn in as the governor of Anambra State. Obi, his major opponent in that election, could not understand the action of the electoral commission. As a private sector person who had played no role in politics before his 2003 appearance, Obi could not but shudder at the manipulation that produced Ngige as governor. As a trained financial analyst, Obi understood so much the arithmetic of figures. He was convinced that the figures that produced Ngige as governor did not add up. Consequently, he rejected the sleight of hand and approached the courts to seek redress.

When Obi took his case to the election petitions tribunal, many people winked at the step he had taken. They felt that it was a waste of time for him to look up to the courts for justice. People felt this way because election petitions were not known to yield useful results in the courts. What used to happen was that any petitioner who shows signs of seriousness is usually not allowed to go the whole hog. He would normally be approached by the respondent at some point. A certain understanding would be reached, and the matter will eventually be withdrawn.

It was thought that the Peter Obi legal disputation with Ngige would follow this familiar path. While the case was on, Obi was approached by many to let the sleeping dog lie. He was prevailed upon to withdraw the case. Some, including the clergy, told him to discontinue with the case because, as they told him, whatever that happened in that election was the will of God. But Obi rejected that cheap resort to fatalism. He queried its veracity. He did not believe that God sanctioned the electoral fraud that denied him his governorship victory. Based on this strong conviction, Obi pushed ahead with the case. After nearly three years of litigation, the Enugu Division of the Court of Appeal declared him as the duly elected governor of Anambra State in the 2003 election. Ngige was, consequently, removed as the governor of Anambra State.

The Peter Obi victory at that time was rare. But he achieved that feat because he believed strongly in the court as the bastion of democracy. Obi was driven by a strong sense of justice. His pursuit of this ideal was single-minded. He believed that a country that will make progress must play by the rules. There should be no manipulation. There should be no suppression and subversion of truth.

I was encouraged by and enamoured of Obi's feat. He was later to emerge as THE SUN Man of the Year in 2006. I was one of the editors of THE SUN at that time that considered Obi fit for the position. He became my role model. Significantly, Obi's tenure as the governor of Anambra State turned out to be a model to aspire to. He brought uncommon prudence to bear in governance. He gave public office a bright face and a good name. After eight eventful years, Obi left office in a blaze of glory. He left Anambra state richer and better. His good example drove me into action. I was encouraged by it all. When therefore I finally stepped out for elective position, my aspiration was to make a remarkable difference that would be a reference point like Obi's. In fact, he was one of the few notable Nigerians in politics that I discussed my political aspiration with. Significantly, he supported me morally and materially.

THE MAN FOR THE JOB

My quest for the House of Representatives seat of my federal constituency began in 2017. It was my year of consultations. I had shared my thoughts on the subject matter with notable individuals, especially those who truly appreciated me for who I am and what I am. A higher percentage of those I consulted favoured the idea of a senatorial quest. Given my cosmopolitan outlook and level of exposure, they reasoned that the upper chamber of the National Assembly would be better suited for what I have to offer.

However, upon further consideration of the issue, I decided on my own to scale down my quest to the House of Representatives. My decision was informed by practical realities. I looked at winning and winnable scenarios. I considered what was involved in the entire scheme. My conclusion was that a senate seat was possible but it would be much more Herculean considering the nature and politics of my senatorial district. In the light of this and related considerations, I settled for the House of Representatives.

I approached my aspiration for a seat in the Green Chambers with utmost seriousness. I was interested in quality representation. I set out to change the face of representation at the National Assembly. To take the message of my aspiration home to my constituents, I embarked upon ward to ward campaign, covering all the 33 wards in my federal constituency. The objective was to keep the leaders and delegates to the primary election abreast of my mission and vision. I wanted them to put merit over and above cheap and unedifying considerations.

My message to my constituents was articulated in my mission statement. An excerpt from it read thus:

" For more than two decades, Dr. Amanze Obi, a public intellectual, has been actively involved in national discourse. He has made seminal contributions in this regard and is easily one of the most quoted public affairs analysts in the country. Dr Obi has the courage of his convictions. He is also passionate about what he writes or says. Many admire him immensely and always look forward to his uncommon interventions on national issues.

"As a patriot who has spent the better part of his career building and shaping the nation, Dr Obi wants to step out into the public arena. He wants to put his national discourses into practice by confronting the issues in the field. He knows the issues and he is desirous of putting his vast knowledge, experience and exposure into practice at the National Assembly. With his eclectic disposition, he promises to elevate national discourse with his uncommon interventions and interjections. Dr Obi is driven by a strong passion- a passion to serve. He envisions an assembly where he will give his people a voice and make them proud through quality representation".

Beyond this extract from my mission statement, I had a campaign address which I randomly delivered at rallies. Aspects of the address read thus:

"I have come here to present myself to you as an aspirant to the House of Representatives. I do so with all sense of responsibility. I differentiate myself from the howlers; from the amorphous crowd; and from those who lay unfounded claim to the throne. I aspire to climb the greasy pole of ambition on the basis of who I am and what I am. I do that with utmost confidence and seriousness. I am happy for who I am. I feel fulfilled in this venture because I know that I am eminently qualified for the job. My pedigree is not in doubt. My background is in the public domain. I know that you know that I can deliver.

"Let me make it clear from the outset. My upbringing abhors ostentation. I am schooled in the world of modesty. My training as a man of letters will not and does not permit me to engage in primitive and obscene displays. In this regard, I will try as much as possible not to talk to you about money. I am not one of those who will flash you cash in the hope that it will buy your conscience. Therefore, I am not here to showcase wealth. Rather, I am here to talk about intellect. That is what will do the job. Not cash. Not ostentation. Not showmanship.

"To be a sound legislator, you need mental alertness. You need to be intellectually savvy. You have to be of sound mind. You have to have character and integrity. And of course, you have to be physically fit. Beyond these, you have to know the world around you. You should be a store house of knowledge. This is what you need to get the job done. Not a load of cash. If cash were to be the essential denominator in this venture, we can as well stray into Ariaria or Ochanja market and make a random selection of non starters and inconsequential backwood men and women to represent us. But that, of course, will be disastrous. We have come near disasters in the past owing to the low acumen of most of those who have represented us. We can no longer afford such expensive gambles. We must move into a redemptive era. An era that will guarantee the people quality representation. I represent this paradigm shift. I have come to wrought a change in the political landscape, believing in the oft-repeated dictum that what is necessary for evil to triumph is for those who know to do nothing. I will do something.

"Why do I sound this confident? I do so because I have, by the grace of God, enjoyed sound education. I have read widely and I have acquired vast knowledge. Besides, I have travelled far and wide. I have mingled with influence. I have interfaced with power. I have joined issues with some of the best brains across the globe. And I have stood tall in their midst. I am only asking you to send me to a familiar turf so that I can play the role that I am very accustomed to.

"I am happy that I have finally come to this point where I stand before you to present myself. I do so with a sense of fulfilment , knowing full well that sending me to the National Assembly is the best choice you can make at this time. You really cannot make a better choice. Do not gamble with your votes. You will be toying with your future if you make a wrong choice. Take a bold step by identifying with the man you can be sure of. The man who knows the issues. The man who will earn the respect and confidence of his peers. I urge you to identify with a national icon, a persuasive speaker and a swift hand who has written himself into stardom. That man is Dr. Amanze Obi- the best man for the job".

It is interesting to note that my campaign messages were well received by my audiences. They resonated with the people. My possible candidature was widely discussed. There was unanimity of opinion that I was, truly, the best man for the job among the pool of aspirants. However, some people did not fail to remind me that the best candidate may not necessary emerge as winner. As a matter of fact, that did not need any emphasis. We have seen a number of quality candidates lose elections in Nigeria on account of primordial and primitive considerations. But I thought that it was necessary and expedient to talk my people out of self-annihilation.

I did not, at the end of the day, win the primary election. The contest went the way of a typical Nigerian election. There were intrigues; there were betrayals; and there was bad blood. Regardless of all this, lessons were learnt. I came out of the contest wiser, at least politically. But the development was very much discussed among my peers and associates. They regretted the fact that our politics was still driven by crass opportunism and primitivity. When on one occasion I met Emma Agu, a professional colleague and former Managing Director of Champion Newspapers, the issue of my election came up for discussion. Emma had this to say: " A society that looks at someone like you and says it does not want you, is that society sane?" The disappointment in his voice was not his alone. It was a measure of our collective failure as a people and as a country.

Chapter 32

PIONEERING THE AHIAJOKU INSTITUTE

The most remarkable event that took place during my one-year stint at the Ministry of Culture and Tourism was the 2010 Ahiajoku festival which was held under my guide as Commissioner. Ahiajoku, an intellectual festival which celebrates Igbo culture, values, civilization and worldview, was instituted in 1979 by the government of the first civilian governor of Imo State, Chief (Dr) Sam Onunaka Mbakwe.

Ambassador Kemjika Anoka, the Director of Culture in Imo State at the time Ahiajoku Lecture Series was instituted, pointed out that the objective of the series is to define aspects of Igbo culture and relate them to the main corpus of Nigerian cultures as well as to African and world civilization. It is also to create a challenging situation for scholars to undertake relevant research on Igbo culture, especially the more basic and fundamental ones, among others. The word 'AHIAJOKU' "is an Igbo conceptual reference to cultivation, fertility and harvest. Yam being the prestige and culturally important crop of the Igbo people that it is, its cultivation and harvesting are traditionally linked with Ahiajoku."[35]

The Igbo, according to Pius Okigbo, "belong to a dietary group normally referred to as the yam culture which extends from Ivory

Coast to the eastern boundary of the Cameroon mountains. It is entrenched in the forest areas of the guinea savannah and has defined the political economy of the Igbo ever since."[36]

Essentially, the lecture series is an annual harvest of thought. It does not only provide the platform for the Igbo to know more about their identity, it involves a dynamic interaction with their environment and their neighbours.

Since 1979 when Prof. MJC Echeruo set the tone for the lectures with his curtain raiser entitled "A Matter of Identity", a number of Igbo scholars have followed suit in the bid to sustain the objectives of the series. However, by 2008, the Ohakim administration rebranded Ahiajoku, moving it away from mere lecture series to a festival. One of the high points of the rebranding was the deliberate shift in the thematic concerns that the lectures explore. From its original and pristine concept of celebrating the yam culture especially as it relates to cultivation, fertility and harvest, the rebranded lectures dwell on contemporary issues that are of immediate relevance to the Igbo and their environment.

The 2008 and 2009 editions were a case in point. While the legendary Chinua Achebe who was the 2008 Ahiajoku lecturer dwelt on the vexed issue of disunity among the Igbo, the 2009 edition delivered by Prof Barth Nnaji, a robotics engineer, focused on the energy crisis that Nigeria faces with a special focus on the Igbo nation.

I was a witness to the new development. My impressions about the new Ahiajoku was captured in an article in the Daily Sun of 2nd February, 2009 entitled " As Ahiajoku Assumes a New Face." It reads thus:

"There is no doubt that the Ahiajoku Lecture Series has remained a huge cultural and intellectual fiesta since it was conceived by the government of Imo State in 1979.

For the 24 times that it has held in its 30-year history, Ahiajoku lecture as a harvest of thoughts never failed to excite. That is why many have continued to recall with relish some of the very seminal deliveries such as M.J.C. Echeruo's " Ahamefule: A Matter of Identity"(1979); Adiele Afigbo's "The Age of Innocence"(1981); and Pius Okigbo's "Towards a Reconstruction of the Political Economy of Igbo Civilization"(1986), among others.

"But at no time has the idea been made to assume a deeper and more relevant dimension than the 2008 edition which held on January 23, 2009. Riding on the springboard of the well-oiled "New Face of Imo"- the defining character and characteristic of the Ikedi Ohakim administration in Imo State, the Ahiajoku festival was made to take on a new life that promises to herald a new dawn in the quest by the Igbo for greater relevance and fulfilment. That was why the event deviated from what used to be the norm. Rather than the one-day event it has always been, the festival was programmed as a week-long event that reflected variously and copiously on different aspects of Igbo being and knowing, culminating in the lecture that was delivered by Prof. Chinua Achebe.

"But what has been the place of Ahiajoku in Igbo cultural and intellectual renaissance since its inception in 1979? To answer this question, let us recall that the Government of Imo State led by Chief Sam Mbakwe had, on 30th November, 1979, given birth to the Ahiajoku Lecture Series. It was designed as a pan-Igbo intellectual wellspring aimed at highlighting and redefining the position and contribution of the Igbo to the growth and development of the world. Coming barely nine years after the Biafran War that decapitated the Igbo and left them mentally shattered, Ahiajoku was an idea whose timing was relevant and germane. It provided the atmosphere for Igbo reflection and possible rejuvenation. It was a revivalist strategy to buoy up the sagged and demented spirit of the Igbo. Through it, Igbo scholars woke their peers up from imposed and inevitable slumber and got the people to worry less about Nigeria and situate themselves, instead, in the context of world affairs.

"So far, the idea has paid off. Even though the Igbo were not lacking in the idea of who they are and the contributions they have made and continue to make to world civilization, the yearly gathering has illuminated these issues better and sharpened their focus on them.

"But it does appear that the Igbo are not content with mere theoretical issues such as the ones that Ahiajoku highlights. Having taken the Igbo through the labyrinth of intellectual and cultural rediscovery, the new thinking is that some attention should be paid to how the intellectual harvest can be used to bring about technological and scientific developments that will make the Igbo truly relevant in a world that is largely driven by technological and scientific innovations. This is the practical approach the new government in Owerri wants to bring to bear on the cultural event. This objective was brought to the fore by the week-long deliberations that have just ended in Owerri. The challenge then is to imbibe this new strategy and work towards the objective that has been highlighted.

"The philosophy of development which the government of Imo State is seeking to bring to the Ahiajoku lecture series is one that should permeate Igbo effort to stay in the limelight in world affairs. It is the crisis of this new thinking that also faces the World Igbo Congress (WIC) which was conceived in Houston, Texas, United States of America, in 1994. After operating for more than 10 years as a Diaspora idea aimed at giving the Igbo nation a new impetus in a hostile Nigerian setting, the WIC has had cause, in recent years, to reexamine its strategies. The Congress is under pressure to move away from being an annual gathering for talks and discussions and graduate into a think tank that can point the way for Igbo renaissance and rejuvenation in contemporary

Nigeria. This is the challenge before the congress and any other Igbo organisation or gathering that seeks to stand the test of time. It is the critical juncture which Ahiajoku, WIC, Ohaneze or any other Igbo organisation must get to before its impact can be fully appreciated.

"It is significant to note that Igbo scholars have enriched Igbo thoughts and ideas with the illuminating lectures that they delivered at the various fora - be it at WIC, Ahiajoku or Ohaneze gatherings. But what has been sorely lacking is the will to domesticate these issues, make them as practicable as possible and use same to launch the people and the nation into the much needed industrial, technological and scientific orbit that Igboland desperately needs.

"But it would appear that the main snag that has hindered progress in this regard is the absence of unity that reigns in Igbo circles and affairs. The spirit of individualism which the Igbo are known for is still playing an arresting role in their affairs. Issues that are brought to limelight by individuals are largely ignored and dismissed as the fancies and idiosyncrasies of such individuals by the collective. This tendency is one that has relegated team spirit to the background, making the people to fail woefully where collective effort is required to make an idea work or achieve the desired objective.

In fact, the Igbo are largely cynical when issues that border on collectivism come into play. It was this cynicism, however muted, that greeted Ohakim's seminal lecture in Detroit, Michigan, United States, in 2007 during the occasion of that year's convention of the World Igbo Congress. In the paper, Ohakim had come up with a highly brilliant idea -that of mega city for South East Nigeria. The idea was well received and applauded by the Congress. But when we returned to Nigeria, most of those who were supposed to think through the idea and give it impetus or support merely sneered at it. They dismissed it as the fancies of one man which they would not be bothered about.

Things go this way in Igbo circles owing to lack of unity. The people and their governments are dangerously individualistic. Perhaps, it was in recognition of this debilitating tendency that Achebe left the path of intellectualism which the previous lectures of Ahiajoku had treaded and chose, instead, to preach unity among the Igbo.

As the wise one, Achebe must have taken a dispassionate look at the problem of the Igbo and may have located it largely in the disunity that exists among the people. That was why he disappointed those who may have whetted their appetite in expectation of intellectual erudition from Achebe. He must have noticed that much of this had been done in the past by the 23 lecturers that featured in the Ahiajoku series from 1979 to 2007.

"Whereas the previous lectures may have explored Igbo worldview and relevance in contemporary world to the fullest, little or no attention was paid to the all-important unity question which the Igbo have failed to answer since they emerged from the ruins of war. The need to address the unity question becomes even more imperative considering the fact that disunity among the Igbo is largely a post-Civil War phenomenon. It was after the war, for instance, that the Igbo-speaking people of Rivers State began to disclaim their igboness in preference for non-Igbo identities. The same Igbo denial exists in some Igbo-speaking areas of Delta State.

"It is significant to note that some of the anti-Igbo sentiments which the Igbo of Rivers State and, to some extent, Delta State harbour against their kith and kin from what is today known as South East Nigeria derive largely from differences in dialects.

It was the problem of disunity occasioned largely by discrimination such as this that Achebe preached against. It was an apt occasion to do so.

"Essentially, the new face of the Ahiajoku lecture tends towards a shift in focus. From the rebranding that the Imo State Government has brought to bear on it to the practical issue of Igbo unity which Achebe emphasized, the festival promises to be the single, most relevant cultural cum intellectual event that the Igbo nation can boast of. What is needed now is the sustenance of the new face and dimension which the lecture series has come to assume."[37]

From being a witness in the 2008 and 2009 editions, I became not just a participant but the key driver of the 2010 edition delivered by Prof Chinedu Nebo. He reflected on the topic, " Nigerian Sectoral Underdevelopment and Leadership Challenge: The Igbo Perspective". His lecture was particularly rich in the sense that it incorporated all the ingredients of rebranding that the festival underwent under Ohakim.

Another thing that marked the 2010 Ahiajoku Lecture out was that it held at a sprawling ultra modern complex which was then putatively called "New Multipurpose Hall".

After hosting the epochal 2010 Ahiajoku Lecture, the complex which was then at its completion stage came to assume a life of its own. It had become evident, going by the architectural masterpiece that it is, that the complex was more than a mere multipurpose hall. Consequently, it became expedient to accord it the full status it deserves.

As the serving Commissioner in the relevant government department, I, in consultation with the Governor, considered it appropriate to name and call the complex "Ahiajoku Convention Centre". To give official effect to this idea, I sponsored a memo at the Executive Council proposing the renaming of the complex as proposed. The Council approved the memo and the complex became known as Ahiajoku Convention Centre.

With this development, the governor thought it wise to institutionalize the lecture series. Consequently, the Ahiajoku

Institute was born. The institute was part of the rebranding process that the lecture series underwent under the Ohakim administration.

Ohakim had lofty plans for the Institute in the life of his administration. But his loss of his re-election bid altered all of that. He lost the opportunity to put in place his beautiful dreams for the Institute. That notwithstanding, he ensured that the idea did not die with the end of his administration. Thus, a few weeks before he left office, he appointed a Director General for the Institute. The lot of the appointment fell on me.

Ohakim made the appointment knowing full well that he was leaving office. Having institutionalized the Lecture Series, he took it for granted that the administration that was taking over from his would uphold and sustain the creation of the Institute. But that was not to be. His successor threw the Institute and whatever idea that was behind it overboard. The result was that the Institute never took off.

Chapter 33

A TOUCHSTONE FOR THE FESTIVAL

Following the unplanned exit of Ohakim, Imo suddenly found itself in the hands of a governor who knew neither method nor order. Rochas Okorocha, Ohakim's successor, was a whimsical personality. He knew no system. He respected no system. Under him, Imo was governed on ad hoc basis. His governance style, as unconventional as it was, caused a lot of disquiet and consternation in the state. The people never, before Okorocha, saw a governor who did not play by the rules.

Given this state of affairs, the election of Emeka Ihedioha as the governor of Imo State was a momentous event. It got Imo quaking. His victory heralded a new day. It was fresh and refreshing. It put the people in a celebratory mood. For the people of Imo state, the victory was akin to a supernatural intervention. It was as if the god from the machine, as we know it in ancient Greek theatre, has providentially been introduced into the Imo situation.

Why did the people of Imo state feel that way? They did so not because they never imagined that an Ihedioha would ever emerge as their governor but because they felt a sense of relief. They felt rescued from the vice grip of Rochas Okorocha. Under him, the people, before their very eyes, were reduced to helpless spectators.

The Okorocha government was, at best, a one-man dance drama and at worst, a family concert in which the dramatis personae repeated their roles for want of diversity. The people for whose sake the government existed had no say and no input.

The people's subjugation under the Okorocha governorship was bad enough. But what rankled the most was the governor's decision to instal his son-in-law as his successor. When Okorocha came up with this idea, the people of Imo thought that it was a mere gimmick. They considered it unimaginable. They thought that he was merely testing the waters. But what started as mere theatrics played to the receptive audience of some party faithful was to blossom into an out of stage concert. It was real. It became a big issue. For the people, the gambit was a jolt. It was an assault on their sobriety. They could not come to terms with it. The effrontery was too much for them to ignore. The audacity was bemusing. The idea sounded like a story from a book. The people did not know what to make of it. They thought they were in a trance. How will this bad dream end? That was the state of affairs until rescue came their way through the governorship election of 2019. That explains the goodwill that heralded the emergence of Ihedioha as governor. The development had epical dimensions. It is a story that will be told over and over again for a long time to come.

How did Imo come about this harvest? The turn of the century has brought with it a crop of enthusiasts who hankered after a new political culture that will move our politics away from its threadbare and anaemic tradition. Ihedioha was one of them. But he went beyond enthusiasm. He did not allow the momentum to define him. Rather, he was guided by a thought process; a plan of action. His period of tutelage was as eventful as it could be. It provided him with an opportunity to construct his own system. The clout and knowledge that flowed from it eventuated in his ascension to the Lower Chamber of the National Assembly.

While at the National Assembly, he did not dissolve into anonymity as was the case with most of his peers. Rather, he continued to learn and network on the job. Whereas many of those who started off with him ended up as provincial experts, Ihedioha was more focused on national politics. In no time, he gathered a lot of moss. He achieved the most uncommon when he won election for three consecutive times to the House of Representatives. He did not bungle the opportunity. Instead, he reaped bountifully from it. The result was his rise to the coveted office of Deputy Speaker of the House of Representatives. But he was not just a deputy speaker, he was a very visible and influential one. So far, he has remained the most recognised and respected deputy speaker of the House of Representatives from 1999 till date.

It was on the strength of this national clout and exposure that he set sail. While at the National Assembly, he had begun to dream dreams. Imo, his home state, was on his mind. He acknowledged the fact that some of those who have had the privilege of presiding over the affairs of the state meant well and also tried their level best in the effort to develop the state. He was also aware that some others were on a mission of plunder and open air thievery. But he was not going to dwell on the past. Rather, he envisioned a new Imo where life will be more abundant. He is a modern day utilitarian who, like Jeremy Bentham, is out to provide the greatest good for the greatest number. He brought his mission home in his political manifesto entitled "Together We Will Rebuild Imo", when he declared that his governorship quest was pivotal to the future development of Imo State. He pledged thus: " If am elected, I solemnly promise that I shall enhance the standard of governance, ensure the security of lives and property of our people, raise the quality of leadership, promote the principles of democracy and uphold the rule of law." He was guided by this when he declared to stand election to the office of governor of Imo state. The expectation was that Imo would be better under him as he set out to dance to the rhythms of destiny.

No sooner was he elected into office than he came up with bright, new ideas. One of them was his vision for the institutionalization of the Ahiajoku Lecture Series. Before him, the idea of the Institute existed, but with him, the Institute became a reality. He created the Ahiajoku Institute and appointed me the Director General. As someone who has had so much to do with Ahiajoku affairs before the appointment, I helped the governor to fashion out what the Ahiajoku Institute should be.

By its very conception, Ahiajoku Institute is an elevation and broadening of the annual Ahiajoku Lecture Series. Broadly speaking, the Ahiajoku Institute was conceived as an extra- ministerial department established by the Government of Imo State for the purposes of harnessing all the cultural activities of the state. It is fashioned like the Goethe Institute- the German cultural association- and Instituto Italiano De Cultura- the Italian cultural Institute.

Its focus includes, but not limited to, the following:

1. Organising the annual Ahiajoku lecture series.
2. Providing a programme of cultural events for the state and ensuring that the state's cultural potentials are properly harnessed and celebrated.
3. Engagement in cultural diplomacy by promoting the study of Igbo language and culture abroad as well as encouraging international cultural exchanges and relations.
4. Serve as storehouse for information about Igbo civilization, culture and society.
5. It is a centre for the exchange of films, music, theatre and literature.
6. It is a vehicle for the celebration of other artistic forms such as Mbari.

7. It is a research institute on culture. In this regard, it is to gather, collate and publish in book form cultural milestones in Igboland, including the Ahiajoku lectures.

In essence, the Instiute was positioned to be the intellectual resource base of not only Imo State, but also that of a larger Nigeria.

With this broad concept, the Institute took off under my directorship. But the road to its formation and take-off was not an easy one. As a new creation, the Institute had no structures except the ones that I struggled to put in place. With absolutely nothing in place to work with, I had to go the extra mile to ensure that the Institute took off in earnest. But what helped my drive was that the governor who took the bold step to create the Institute meant well. He wanted it to succeed. Thus, within the few months that the Institute operated, we were able to put in place structures and systems that made the Institute an instant success.

It is noteworthy that the institutionalization of the lecture series came at a time the festival was in its 40th year. For the Institute and for the government, this was a milestone that must not be glossed over. That was especially so considering the fact that the lecture series was abandoned by the Rochas Okorocha administration for seven years. The last Ahiajoku lecture took place in 2012 before its resuscitation by the Ihedioha administration. Consequently, the 2019 Ahiajoku lecture was not just about the return of a festival which the people cherish so much, it was also a celebration of 40 years of the lecture series. To give effect to the anniversary, Prof. MJC Echeruo, who delivered the inaugural lecture in 1979, was invited to also give the anniversary lecture.

Echeruo's lecture entitled: "OGU ERI MBA: We Shall Survive", was something of a homecoming. After 40 years of meandering through the intellectual minefield in the quest by the Igbo to situate their being and knowing properly in the context of world affairs,

Echeruo, the man who first picked up the gauntlet 40 years earlier, was the right man to look back in time. How have the Igbo fared in the quest? Are they in the right track or are they wandering aimlessly? Echeruo provided copious answers to the nagging questions that beset the Igbo. But he was unequivocal on one issue. The Igbo should jettison their romance with a possible Jewish connection. Instead, they should look inwards and homewards. Therein lies the true Igbo history and identity.

The anniversary lecture was the first major engagement of the newly created Ahiajoku Institute. And Echeruo, the man who was there at the beginning, was delighted to be associated with the Institute.

In his address at the 40th anniversary of the lecture series, Ihedioha succinctly situated the idea behind the Institute. He said:

"The 2019 Ahiajoku Festival, certainly, marks another milestone in the "Rebuild Imo Agenda" of the present Imo State Government. Less than a month into this administration, we successfully revived this important element of the Imo State Brand. It was elevated to the status of an Institute overseen by a Director General. This is with a view to making the event a first class resource centre on Igbo culture and civilization like the Goethe Institut- the German cultural association- and Instituto Italiano De Cultura- the Italian cultural institute. We hope that with this structure in place, the Festival would now have an enduring institutional framework.

"The Institute would also drive the implementation of the actionable resolutions of the conferences as well as serve as a veritable institutional memory. At its full bloom, it will be a centre for the production and exchange of films, music, theatre and literature. Furthermore, it would serve as a vehicle for the celebration of other Igbo artistic forms like Mbari. In this regard, it will gather, collate and publish in book and electronic formats cultural milestones, including the Ahiajoku Lectures."38.

With this extra package, the 2019 Ahiajoku Festival turned out to be an epochal event. It was rich in content and output. The celebration provided us with the opportunity to look back and assess how far Ahiajoku has come. It attracted the best of the Igbo, far and near. Apart from the lecture itself, other aspects of the festival, particularly the Colloquium, provided scholars and thinkers of various persuasions the opportunity to ventilate their views on the Igbo condition and the Nigeran state. The huge success which the 2019 Ahiajoku Festival recorded was a pointer to the path of excellence which the Ihedioha administration was treading.

But a whimper trailed the celebration. After the festival, it was clear to one and all that Ihedioha had stolen the show. He had taken Ahiajoku to a new height. He was applauded by people of goodwill. But revisionists were ill at ease with the development. For the first time in the history of Ahiajoku festival, a few misguided fellows began to throw jibes. They began to question the relevance of the all-important festival. At this point, it became obvious that some elements in Igbo circles have lost their bearing. They have become aliens to their own culture and environment . How can a full blooded Igbo soul not be able to appreciate Ahiajoku for what it represents in Igbo cosmology and worldview?

I was full of pity for critics of the the Ahiajoku festival when they, petulantly, associated the celebration with the Biafran agitation. That was a piece of blackmail aimed at giving the Ihedioha administration a bad name before the federal authorities. But they were not supposed to be taken seriously and nobody did. Ahiajoku came into existence nine years after Biafra. At no time did anybody associate the celebration with separatist agitation. There was no reason to do so then. There is also no reason to do so now. It was a case of trying to give a dog a bad name in order to hang it.

We jeered at their folly. But little did we know that their unfounded criticism was a ploy. It was part of the grand plot to rewrite history. Their grouse with Ahiajoku was just a teaser. The real deal was that they had plotted to remove Ihedioha from office. Exactly 45 days after the Ahiajoku festival, the Supreme Court of Nigeria removed Ihedioha from office in very controversial circumstances.

Postscript

JONATHAN AS FALL GUY

In the last one year of the Jonathan presidency, I was, together with a few professional colleagues, privileged to be having interactive sessions with the president on a fairly regular basis. By that time, Jonathan's first tenure was in its last vestiges and frenetic efforts were being made to ensure his reelection for a second term. Given the groundswell of opposition propaganda which his administration had to contend with, the president needed a lot of corrective impulse to be able to weather the storm.

But while some of us hatched strategic intervention mechanisms that were targeted at getting the president to ride the crest, the man did not, from my own assessment, think that there was any urgency to the task ahead. Whereas some of us were, to a reasonable extent, aware of the land mines that the president faced, the man himself was somewhat relaxed about the entire matter. But his unperturbed state did not bother on waning interest in the office he occupied. The fact of the matter was that Jonathan was confident that he was going to win reelection and therefore did not need to fret to retain his seat. In building his confidence, he relied a great deal on the results of the 2011 presidential elections. From time to time, he would review his state-by-state performance in that election, after which he would express confidence that 2015 would not be any less promising.

He was right to a very large extent. He had every chance of winning through popular votes in majority of the states of the federation as was the case in 2011. He had, in four years, given governance a human face. He had done very well in many indices of governance. Besides, his main challenger carried a lot of baggage and was therefore not expected, by any magical acrobatics, to snatch victory from the incumbent.

However, while Jonathan was making reasoned assumptions and conclusions, little did he know that some of his trusted allies were in league with the opposition. By that time, for instance, the loyalty of the INEC chairman, Attahiru Jega, had become doubtful. The opposition APC had become very comfortable with him, and applauded his actions. The PDP government which appointed him only complained. The party through which grace he got appointed had lost him to the opposition. All of this was clear from Jega's actions and utterances. Given this ugly set-up, it was thought that Jonathan would wield the big stick. But he was obviously not going to do that. I was personally worried about having Jega as the umpire for that election. But the president saw things differently. One day, while we were having our normal session with him, I made bold to ask him whether he would allow Jega to conduct the 2015 election. His response was predictable. He would let Jega be because his removal at that time would cause a stir in international and local circles . He said that his detractors, both within and outside our shores, would cash in on that and accuse him of plotting to win by all means. The president did not want to win by all means. He wanted to win in a free and fair manner.

Regrettably, while the president was playing fair and decent politics, he did not do much to stop the hawks from preying on him. Thus, while he would not do untoward things to remain in office, he did not stop the major actors on the opposite end of the spectrum from subverting the system and turning the table against him. From the way it turned out then, it should be taken for granted that the most momentous political event that has taken place in Nigeria since the return of democratic governance to Nigeria in 1999 is the defeat of President Goodluck Jonathan in the 2015 presidential election. The defeat of incumbency at the presidency is an uncommon development in our shores. Nigeria did not have a history of it until Jonathan ushered us into that rare possibility.

Jonathan, Nigeria's president from 2010 to 2015, was a child of circumstance. He was one man who seemed to have a pact with Fortune. His ascendancy to the office of governor of Bayelsa state as well as that of the Vice President of Nigeria was without struggle. Fortune simply smiled at him and he found himself occupying the coveted offices. The same thing was true of his ascendancy to the presidency. His boss, president Umaru Musa Yar'Adua, had taken ill and had to travel out of the country to seek medical attention. Nigerians thought at first that the president's absence was going to be short-lived. But that was not the case. Weeks rolled into months and yet the president did not return. The president's absence slowed down the pace of governance. It brought about an untold lull. Then, tongues began to wag. Nigerians wanted to know the true state of health of their president. But those who were in the know were not willing to intimate Nigerians with the true situation. This created anxiety and tension in the land.

The matter was not helped by the fact that Yar'Adua did not transmit power to the Vice President as required by the constitution apparently because he did not know that he was going to be away for too long. The uncertain state of affairs had a telling effect on the governance of the country. Jonathan, the Vice President, could not do the job of the president because he was not authorized to do so. As the situation dragged on, every other thing was almost brought to a halt. The country was on tenterhooks. A certain cabal was operating underground. The lacuna created by the absence of the president and the inactivity of the Vice President who was forced to maintain a lame duck position was to the advantage of the cabal. They cashed in on the situation and held the country by the jugular. The situation presented the country with a dilemma. What should be done? No solution was in sight as the mafia group frustrated every effort to rescue Nigeria from their vice grip. The country continued to screech along the rough highway until the National Assembly came up with an idea. It invoked the Doctrine of Necessity. The doctrine is the basis upon which extra-legal actions by state actors , which are designed to restore order, are bound to be constitutional. It was applied in Nigeria in 2010 to validate extra-constitutional issues that fall outside the purview of the constitution but are necessary. It was the invocation of this doctrine on 13th February, 2010 that made it possible for Jonathan to assume the role of acting president and was then able to exercise the executive role of the president. Not too long after Jonathan's ascension to the presidential seat, Yar'Adua died and Jonathan became the substantive president.

Riding on the crest of the goodwill which he enjoyed at the time, Jonathan stood for election in February 2011. He won. It was remarkable that that the 'boy' from the creeks of Niger Delta with a lowly parental background and who had no shoes while growing up has made it to the presidency. This feat resonated across the land. The story it told was that if Jonathan could become president, any other Nigerian of humble parentage could also become president of the country.

Having won his own election, Nigerians expected Jonathan to step out of his cocoon and assert his authority as president. But that was hardly the situation. The man remained ensconced in borrowed plumes. He was too reluctant to be the real president that Nigerians voted for. In no time, Nigerians began to see him as a weakling. They began to see him as one president that can easily be tele-guided. He never talked tough. He never acted tough. In extreme cases, he was dismissed as clueless and spineless.

Jonathan was still grappling with this unsavoury image of himself when Boko Haram, the international terrorist organisation, complicated matters for him the more. The group attacked many public property, notably the United Nations building and the headquarters of the Nigeria Police both in Abuja. It also attacked worship centres such as St. Theresa's Catholic Church, Madalla, Niger State. All of these led to loss of many lives and destruction of property. Nigerians cried foul. There was pressure on Jonathan to step up the fight against Boko Haram. To ensure that the bloodletting did not continue , Jonathan was prepared to be tutored on how best to fight terrorism . It was in the midst of all this that some northern elements cajoled him into believing that he committed a security faux pas by making a southerner, Matthew Owoeye Azazi , the National Security Adviser (NSA). They told Jonathan that a southerner had never occupied that office before. They sold the dummy to him that if he appointed a northerner the NSA, Boko Haram would be decimated in no time. Jonathan bought into the blackmail and removed Azazi, his kinsman from Bayelsa state, as the NSA. He was replaced by Col. Sambo Dasuki (rtd.) from Sokoto state. It was in this way that the north infiltrated the Jonathan presidency and dictated the tone and direction of the administration.

Even though Jonathan did so much to give every segment of the country a sense of belonging, he did much more for the north. He built Almajiri schools for them. He established nine federal universities and located six in the north, leaving the south with only three. This is in spite of the fact that the south needed the universities more than the north considering the pressure on existing universities in the south. We have a long list of Jonathan's pro-north policies under his administration. All of this was done so that the north would be favourably disposed to his second term bid in 2015. But the countdown to the 2015 general elections presented us with a curious mix of intrigues. The north had begun to feel, rightly or wrongly, that it has been cheated by the south. It felt that the return of a southerner to the presidential seat too soon after Obasanjo's eight-year rule was not in the best interest of the north. Consequently, the region began to plot Jonathan's fall. But this was not known to the president. To expand the dragnet of the plot, the northern establishment began to scout for an ally in the south. In this matter, Jonathan's south south zone was never to be factored into the plot. It was taken for granted that the president's geo-political zone would not work against him. The only two zones that could be approached were the south east and the south west. But like the south south, the south east was seen as an unfavourable zone with which to plot against Jonathan. The south east, from all indications, adopted Jonathan as their own son. They romanced with his name, Ebele (Ebelemi in Ijaw) and adapted it into Igbo. They also called him Azikiwe. In no time, Jonathan became known as Goodluck Ebele Jonathan (GEJ). It was a fitting sobriquet and it was romanticised for as long as Jonathan was in office. Besides, the Igbo adopted Jonathan to prove to their eastern minority brothers who had always resented the Igbo over the ballyhooed spectre of Igbo domination that the Igbo mean no harm and are ready to give them their due. The Jonathan presidency was an opportunity for the Igbo to demonstrate this goodwill and they did so to the fullest. Given this set-up, the south east was not considered a friendly zone to do business with in the plot against Jonathan.

On the contrary, the south west looked like a fertile ground and the north quickly went fishing there. Using the instrumentality of the newly registered APC, the north, subtly, went into a political alliance with the south west. Bola Tinubu, the political leader of the Yoruba, was coopted for this purpose. An understanding was reached to give the vice presidency to the south west so that it would give unalloyed support to the northern presidential candidate under the APC arrangement. It was on the basis of this arrangement that Nigeria went into the 2015 elections. But again, Jonathan did not see the plot. He still operated as a pan-Nigerian president who has affected every section of the country positively, and would therefore win election for a second term as he did in his first attempt.

It was on the strength of his trust and unsuspecting disposition that Jonathan retained most northerners in critical positions as the 2015 elections approached. The most prominent of them all was Attahiru Jega. It was known to every watcher of our polity at that time that Jega would undo Jonathan if he was allowed to conduct the 2015 elections. The signs were all there. The permanent voter cards (PVCs) which Jega said he would use for the elections were not properly distributed. An overwhelming majority of the cards at that time, were in the hands of northerners. The south complained to no avail while the president watched with astonishing detachment. Besides, Jega's INEC created more voting centres in the countdown to the elections and allocated about 70 percent of them to the north. In fact, the north had a long list of conspirators who were united in their resolve to see to the ouster of Jonathan. All this portended danger for the Jonathan presidency. But he chose to treat them with kid gloves.

The plot from the south west came in a different guise. The zone was somewhat uncomfortable with Jonathan's brotherly disposition towards the south east. The overriding feeling in Yoruba circles at that time was that the Igbo, according to a Yoruba public affairs commentator, were eating with all ten fingers under the Jonathan presidency. The impression therefore was that the Igbo were getting more than their fair share of the national cake under the Jonathan political dispensation. A good number of the Yoruba resented this. For the Yoruba therefore, a vice presidential slot dangled before them by the north was a big carrot. It excited them. They therefore joined forces with the north to ensure the fall of Jonathan. But it is significant to note that the Igbo did not shift ground. They remained with Jonathan even when it seemed to some people that their insistence on and support for Jonathan was a miscalculation. But it was not.

NOTES AND REFERENCES

1. Wikipedia: Power and Authority/ Introduction to Sociology- Lumen Learning.
2. Wikipedia: Lord Acton (1887), Acton-Creighton Correspondence on the theme: Presidents, Kings, Tyrants and Despots.
3. Wikipedia: Brainy Quote.
4. Greene, Robert (1998), The 48 Laws of Power, Profile Books, London, p.xxi.
5. Ibid., p.xxiii.
6. Lyons, J. (1977), Semantics, vol. 11, C.U.P, London, pp. 607-609.
7. Lyons, J. (1981), Language and Linguistics: An Introduction, C.U.P, London, pp. 301-305.
8. Ibid., p.308.
9. Adetugbo, A. (1986), "Nigerian English and the Native English Conventions of Politeness", in Lagos Review of English Studies, Vol. Viii, pp.57-58.
10. Fromklin, V. etal (1978), An Introduction to Language, Holt, p.278.
11. THISDAY, The Sunday Newspaper, October 5, 1997, pp. 4-5.
12. Labov, William, (1972), The Logic of Non-Standard English, The University of Pennsylvania Press, Philadelphia.
13. Sheridan, R.B, (1968), The Rivals, Oxford University Press, Oxford.
14. Third Eye Daily, August 22, 1995, p. 9.
15. THE SUN, June 26, 2003, p.7.
16. THE SUN, August 18, 2003, p.48.
17. WEEKLY SPECTATOR, November 13, 2005, p.34.

18. THISDAY, September 5, 2000, p.40
19. THISDAY, April 2, 2000, p.40.
20. Address by His Excelency, the Executive Governor of Sokoto State, Alhaji Attahiru Dalhatu Bafarawa (Garkuwan Sokoto), on the occasion of a meeting with prominent indigenes of Sokoto State as part of activities marking the three years anniversary of his administration, May, 2002.
21. THISDAY, September 19, 2000, p.40.
22. DAILY SUN, May 7, 2007, p.48.
23. Wikipedia: The Jewish Virtual Library.
24. SATURDAY CHAMPION, October 10, 2009, p.15.
25. SUNDAY SUN, March 29, 2009, p.56.
26. THISDAY, July 21, 2009, p.21.
27. THE NATION, August 3, 2009, p.48.
28. DAILY CHAMPION, August 4, 2009, p.48.
29. DAILY CHAMPION, August 5, 2009, p.48.
30. SUNDAY CHAMPION, August 9, 2009, p.20.
31. Ibid., August 9, 2009, p. 17.
32. NATIONAL LIFE, August 9, 2009, p.10.
33. THE NATION, August 11, 2009, p.20.
34. DAILY CHAMPION, August 17, 2009, p.11.
35. Anoka, Kemjika. "Citation on Ahiajoku Lectures", Ed. Chris Asoluka & Johnson Okafor, " NDIGBO: A MATTER OF IDENTITY: A Collection of 30 Years of Ahiajoku Lecture Series", Volume 1, Lagos, El- Machi Limited, 2009, pp.xi-xii.
36. Okigbo, Pius. "Towards A Reconstruction of the Political Economy of Igbo Civilization", Ed. Chris Asoluka & Johnson Okafor, op. cit. P.279.
37. DAILY SUN, February 2, 2009, p.56.
38. Address by the Governor of Imo State, His Excellency, Rt. Hon. Emeka Ihedioha, CON, Ksc, on the 40th Anniversary of Ahiajoku Lecture Series, at Ahiajoku Convention Centre, Owerri, Saturday, November 30, 2019.

ABOUT THE BOOK

SCENTS OF POWER is a peep through the multiple doors that the author has passed in the course of his career. The account is a product of history. Guided by historical actuality, the author focuses on factuality, authenticity and the true value of knowledge in his reflections about the past. There is no myth or legend in the book. What we have is living history. Even though the author tries to navigate the book out of the realm of autobiography, he, nonetheless, embarks upon a historical narrative that pieces together the rudiments of yesterday and converts them into raw materials for present engagement. The blend is uncommon. It exemplifies and highlights the eclectic bent of the author as an accomplished raconteur.

His adoption of the historical approach in his narrative is significant. It has helped to identify the author as an artist with a significant past and a predisposition to write in a certain manner. This knowledge enables the reader to ascertain how the book reflects the historical forces that shaped it. It has also enabled us to understand how the historical moment upon which the book is anchored produced the moving tale that the author has told. This knowledge guides us into acknowledging the fact that the author's experiences in whatever field he has traversed are not his alone. Instead, they have a universal appeal that makes the account not just the author's story, but everyone's story.

ABOUT THE AUTHOR

Dr. Amanze Obi, scholar, writer and journalist, was educated at the University of Lagos. He spent eleven unbroken years in the university and bagged multiple degrees, capping it with a doctorate in English. He taught in the Department of English of the University of Lagos in the early years of his career.

A frontline journalist and celebrated columnist with over three decades of media exposure, Obi has worked with major Nigerian newspapers where he held senior editorial positions. His weekly newspaper column, BROKEN TONGUES, is easily the toast of perceptive readers.

Obi was, at various times, Commissioner for Information and Strategy as well as that of Culture and Tourism in Imo State. He was also the pioneer Director General of the Ahiajoku Institute, the think tank on Igbo worldview and civilization. He is the author of PERSPECTIVES IN INTERNATIONAL POLITICS (1998) and DELICATE DISTRESS: An Interpreter's Account of the Nigerian Dilemma (2013).

NAME INDEX

Abacha, Sani (General), 31, 87, 174
Abiola, M.K.O. (Chief), 93, 173
Abubakar, Atiku, (Vice
 President), 97
Achebe, Chinua, (Prof.), 196, 197
Aduba, Okagbue, 33
Aduma, John Odey., 29
African National Congress
 (ANC), 75
Agbaso, Martin, 107
Agu, Emma, 194
Akinterinwa, Bola A. (Dr), 33, 36
Akporobaro, F.B.O. (Dr), 22
Amafili, Justin, (Mr) 148
Amega, Atsu-Kofi, (Mr), 48, 49
Anaduaka, Tom, 15
Anele, Douglas, (Professor), 3
Anoka, Kemjika, (Ambassador),
 195
Anyanwu, Chris, (Mrs), 16
Anyim, Anyim Pius., 92
Ararume, Ifeanyi, 106, 110, 126, 158
Aribisala, Karen King.,
 Dr (Mrs.) 19

Asimobi, Steve, 115
Attah, Judith, (Ambassador), 58
Austin, Jane, 4
Awoniyi, Sunday, (Chief), 95
Awoyinfa, Mike, 62, 65, 71, 73
Azazi, Matthew Owoeye., 215
Azikiwe, Nnamdi, 173

Babalola, E.A., (Dr), 34
Babangida, Ibrahim (General),
 87, 95, 172
Bafarawa, Attahiru Dalhatu.,
 (Alhaji), 92, 93, 110
Beckett, Samuel, 17
Bello, Ahmadu, (Sir), 93
Bio, Julius Maada., 67
Blake, William, 4
Boggs, Patton, 122
Buhari, Muhamadu, General
 (rtd.), 74, 172

Chukwuemeka, Chuk,
 119, 152
Chukwuma, Helen, 23

Clark, Ebun, Dr (Mrs), 20
Clinton, Hillary, 122

Daniel, Muyiwa, 134
Dasuki, Sambo, Col. (rtd.) 215
Diaz, Jose, (Mr), 48
Dubes, J. l., 75

Echeruo, M.J.C. (Prof.), 196, 207
Edah, Rita Ese., 16
Egwu, Sam (Dr), 88, 90, 92
Eko, Ebele, (Professors), 23
Emeka, Ihedioha 203
Enweren, Evan, (Chief), 101
Eruvebetine, A.E. (Professor), 22
Ezeigbo, Akachi, (Professor), 23

Fairfax, Jane, 4
Fayemiwo, Moshood, 7
Firth, J. R., 9 Fox, John, 122
Friedan, Betty, 56

Giwa, Dele, 87
Goebbels, Paul Joseph., 117
Golding, William, 76
Gowon, Yakubu, (General), 95

Hofmann, Barrie, 123
Horn, Robert, 122

Ifijeh, Victor, (Mr), 33
Igwe, Dimgba, (Mr), 62, 141
Ihedioha, Emeka (Rt. Hon.) 203, 204, 205, 207, 208, 209

Ilomuanya, Eze Cletus Ikechukwu, 159
Irechukwu, George, 179
Iwuoha, Chiemeka, 132
Izeze, Emeka, (Mr), 29

Jackson-Lee, Sheila, 120
Jammeh, Yahyah, (President), 66, 69
Jega, Attahiru, 212, 217
Jonathan, Goodluck, (President), 159, 213, 216

Kabbah, Tejan (President), 66, 67, 68, 69
Kabila, Laurent, (President), 36, 37, 46
Kalu, Orji Uzor., (Chief), 60, 72, 88, 132, 135
Kanu, Nwankwo, 90
Kanzas, Thomas, (Professor), 43
Kasavubu, Joseph, 38
Kentebe, Benedict, 3
Koromah, Jonny, 67
Kure, Abulkadir, 88

Labov, William, 54
Lumumba, Patrice, 38
Luthulis, Albert, 75
Lyons, John, 8

Machiavelli, Nicolo, 176
Mandela, Nelson Rolihlahla., 71, 72

Name Index

Mbaga, Etienne, (Mr), 45
Mbakwe, Sam (Chief), 102, 197
Mbakwe, Sam Onunaka. (Dr), 195
Mbaya, Etienne Richard., 40, 47
Mbeki, Thabo, (President), 71, 72
Mobiko, Andre Abeiye. (Mr), 50
Momoh, Joseph, 67
Morrison, Toni, 23
Motlanthe, Kgalema Petrus., 71
Mpoyo, Pierre-Victor (Mr), 38, 47
Mubanga, Muboyayi, (Mr), 50
Mudiay, Oscar (Mr), 44, 45
Mugabe, Robert, (Mr), 48

Nebo, Chinedu, (Prof.), 201
Ngige, Chris, (Dr), 188
Nnaji, Barth, (Prof.), 196
Nnaji, Lawrence Okey., 17
Nnamani, Chimaroke, 88
Nwankwo, Kingsley, 3
Nwosu, Nnamdi, 134
Nwosu, Steve, 62
Nzeakah, Godwin, 133
Nzeribe, Arthur, (Senator), 129, 154, 157, 187

Obaigbena, Nduka, 33, 62
Obama, Barack, 124
Obasanjo, Olusegun, (President), 74, 92, 94, 128, 158
Obasi, Ely, 15
Obi, Amanze, (Dr), 3, 21, 145, 191, 193
Obi, Peter, 188, 189

Obinna, Anthony J.V. (Most Reverend), 168
Odili, Peter, 88
Ogbonnaya, Obasi, 29
Ohakim, Emma, 152
Ohakim, Ikedi, (Governor), 107, 109, 112, 119, 125, 135, 137, 138, 139, 156, 187, 197 Okere, Ethelbert, 117, 143
Okigbo, Pius, 196
Okoro, Luke, 133
Okorocha, Rochas, 160, 203, 207
Okpala, Ngor, 162
Okpareke, Chinedu, (Mr), 152,153
Omatseye, Sam, 132
Onuoha, Chikwem, 111, 118
Onwuekwe, Comfort, (Miss), 55
Onyegbaduo, Pini Jason., 149
Osadolor, Kingsley, 30
Osadolor, Kingsley, (Mr), 30, 183
Otu, John, 88
Otu, John, (Dr), 90

Rasaki, Raji, (Col.), 16
Rimi, Abubakar, (Alhaji), 95

Sankoh, Foday, 67
Saraki, Olusola, (Dr), 95
Seko, Mobutu Sese., (President), 37
Shonekan, Earnest, (Chief), 173
Strasser, Valentine, 67
Sule, Maitama, (Alhaji) 95

Thambos, Oliver, 75
Tinubu, Bola, 216
Tofa, Bashir Othman., 174
Tofa, Uthman (Alhaji), 94
Tomoloju, Ben, 28, 29
Tshisekedi, Etienne, (Mr), 39

Uche, Ogbonnaya, (Chief), 100
Uchegbu, Achilleus, 133
Udenwa, Achike, (Governor), 88, 100, 106, 107, 157

Ugwu, Charles, (Engr.), 158
Umunna, Nze I.M.O., 104

Walker, Alice, 23, 57
Wollstonecraft, Mary, 56

Yar'Adua, Umaru Musa. (Alhaji), 128, 213
Yusuf, M. D., (Alhaji), 95

Zubairu, Tanko, 102

SUBJECT INDEX

Action Congress of Nigeria (ACN), 160
African National Congress (ANC), 75
Ahiajoku Festival, 195
  Institute, 206
  All Peoples Party (APP) 94
  Progressives Grand Alliance (APGA), 160,188
  Progressives Grand Alliance (APGA), 107
Alliance for Democracy (AD) 94
  of Democratic Forces for the Liberation o 40
Almajiri schools, 215

Back Page Column 53
Best Graduating Student, 14
Boko Haram, 215
Broken Tongues, 54, 55, 59, 60, 65

Campus Politics, 7
Champion Newspapers, 194

Civil Rule, 185
Congressional Black Caucus Conference (CBC) 124
Congressional Black Caucus Foundation Inc (CBCF) 119
Culture, 9

Democratic Party (PDP), 94
Deputy Editorial Page Editor, 51
Disc Jockey, 5, 15

Ecomog, 68

Favourable verdicts on thesis, 23
Foreign Affairs Editor, 33, 36
Freetown, 67

Independent National Electoral Commission (INEC), 106, 162

Land of Lincoln, 80
Layabout, 5

National Conference on
    Reconstruction (CNR), 40
    Democratic Coalition
        (NADECO), 174
    Party of Nigeria (NPN), 93
    Republican Convention
        (NRC), 172
Newswatch Magazine, 87
Nigerian Linguistic cultures, 12
Northern People's Congress
    (NPC), 93

Organization of African Unity
    (OAU), 48

Peoples Democratic Party (PDP),
    94, 106, 128, 186
President of English Students
    Association, 8
    of National Association of
        Students of E 8
Progressive Peoples Alliance
    (PPA), 107, 110

Rigour Major, 5
Romantic Hero, 138

Sharia, 97
Social Democratic Party (SDP),
    172

The Guardian Newspapers, 28,
    87, 183
Influencers, 188
Man for the Job, 190
PUNCH, 87
SUN, 61, 63, 64, 67
Sunday Magazine (TSM), 16

United States of America, 78
University of Lagos, 3
    of Lagos Students Union
        (ULSU), 7

Whitney Young Library, 21

www.ingramcontent.com/pod-product-compliance
Lightning Source LLC
Chambersburg PA
CBHW030034100526
44590CB00011B/203